André Louf, ocso

In the School of Contemplation

MONASTIC WISDOM SERIES: NUMBER FORTY-EIGHT

In the School of Contemplation

by

André Louf, ocso

Translated by

Paul Rowe, ocso

α

Cistercian Publications
www.cistercianpublications.org

LITURGICAL PRESS
Collegeville, Minnesota
www.litpress.org

A Cistercian Publications title published by Liturgical Press

Cistercian Publications
Editorial Offices
161 Grosvenor Street
Athens, Ohio 54701
www.cistercianpublications.org

This work was originally published in French as *A L'Ecole de la Contemplation*, © Lethielleux 2004.

Excerpts from documents of the Second Vatican Council are from *Vatican Council II: Constitutions, Decrees, Declarations; The Basic Sixteen Documents*, edited by Austin Flannery, OP, © 1996. Used with permission of Liturgical Press, Collegeville, Minnesota.

Unless otherwise indicated, Scripture texts in this work are translated from the French edition.

3	4	5	6	7	8	9

Library of Congress Cataloging-in-Publication Data

Louf, André.
    [Works. Selections. English]
    In the school of contemplation / by Andre Louf, OCSO ; translated by Paul Rowe, OCSO.
       pages cm. — (Monastic wisdom series ; number forty-eight)
    Compilation of works originally presented in various languages.
    This work was originally published in French as A L'Ecole de la Contemplation, © Lethielleux 2004.
    Includes bibliographical references.
    ISBN 978-0-87907-147-9 — ISBN 978-0-87907-487-6 (ebook)
    1. Monastic and religious life. 2. Spiritual life—Catholic Church.
I. Rowe, Paul, 1971–

BX2435.L68   2015
248.8'94—dc23   2015003759

Contents

Foreword

André Louf (1929–2010) was abbot of the Trappist-Cistercian monastery of Mont-des-Cats in the north of France from 1963 to 1997. He was one of those personalities whose light shines beyond the limited milieu of their own vocations. His books have fed the spiritual lives of numerous Christians, in monasteries and beyond. There was doubtless at work in him something of the same mysterious action of the Spirit already identified, in the distant past, by the Desert Fathers. This is a phenomenon explicitly mentioned on several occasions by André Louf himself when he was questioned about the particular fruitfulness of monastic life.

For many years, André Louf maintained a solid fraternal relationship with the young monastic community of Bose in northern Italy, founded by Enzo Bianchi. Bose had the excellent idea to collect in a single book, published by their Qiqajon Editions, a series of texts by Louf that had previously appeared scattered in various journals (*Collectanea Cisterciensia, Cistercian Studies, Christus, Vie consacrée, Les Amis des monastères*) between 1969 and 1996. These texts include a number of presentations by André Louf at certain monastic meetings, which explains the oral style that has been preserved, as well as the reiteration of certain thoughts and anecdotes from one text to another, the better to clarify the subject at hand. The texts do more than paint a panorama of different aspects of monastic life: they shed light on the deep journey of all monastics and, really, of every authentic seeker after God.

André Louf speaks, with good reason, of different forms of "complicity" between the contemplative life and certain challenges addressed to the Church. With its singular focus, the

monastic experience concentrates within itself the deep movements of the life of the Spirit that are found in every human being
docile to them. Its intensity enables one to better understand,
by means of this experience, what takes place in the encounter
of a human being with the Father and the Son. In this sense, everyone can read the first chapters of this book that focus on the
common life and obedience in the monastery and find there much
to nourish his or her own reflections. One will find there that the
so-called "desert," about which Louf has some striking pages,
exceeds the literal framework of the monastery and deeply affects
every religious and indeed every human experience. Moreover,
if one is willing to be attentive, the "desert" can open one out to
the whole world.

Here the question of ecumenism naturally arises, especially
its link with monastic tradition as understood by Eastern Orthodoxy. It is precisely when we plumb the depths of the Christian mystery that authentic dialogue can take place with all the
delicacy, attentiveness, charity, and humility that it demands.
In this connection, the account that André Louf gives here of a
"pilgrimage" to Mount Athos and some monasteries in Romania
is very expressive.

Finally, the book comes to its completion by way of a return
to the center of the monastic experience, through the liturgy.
One could easily read and reread the beautiful meditation on the
Psalms as a true introduction to praise, as an invitation to enter
into the poetic and creative action by which the Spirit releases all
the potentialities of human speech in the one who prays. Likewise, by revisiting the tradition in this way, Louf introduces his
reader into the dynamism that is at the heart of the liturgy and
yet carries the liturgy beyond itself: the dynamism that is the
work of God's Word.

But this work manifests itself only to someone who gazes upon
God's Word with love. And so the book concludes by making
this point through a brief contemplation of the mystery of Jesus'
death and resurrection. And here, at the end, we find again what
had been underscored by the texts on the common life in the
beginning: namely, that the Word of the Father, which the Son

makes known to us by giving us his life, is in its entirety a gift of mercy, that is to say, a gift of love springing up from the very depths of God.

Jean-François Bouthors
(French edition)

1

Spiritual Experience

How is the life of the Spirit manifested in us, and what criteria do we have for discerning his presence and identifying our experience of him?

You will all agree that this is an important and urgent task in the Church of today. We are being given a lot of new criteria to apply to our spiritual experience—or at least, criteria that are applicable to human experience in general—psychological, sociological, "religious" (using the word in a restricted sense), and even aesthetic.

The great temptation, the great confusion that threatens us here, is that of being satisfied with these attempts and in the end raising to the status of absolute norms and adequate criteria things that only skim the surface of our experience of the Spirit. What we should be engaging in, on the contrary, is a ceaseless effort of confrontation between the light that is in us from the Holy Spirit and the light that comes from profane reflection. It is an effort to meet the adversary and to join battle, and it is the special task of theologians.

We notice nowadays that Christians and even religious are becoming more and more insensitive to the specifically spiritual domain and incapable of truly discerning it. This insensitivity is partly due to the fact that Christians, inadvertently perhaps, are putting their hope in this arsenal of new criteria now at their disposal. On the whole, we in the West are ill-equipped to express our experience of the Spirit even to ourselves, and it is perhaps a good thing that we are only just beginning to try.

Now we are called on to wake up. We must become aware of the reality of the Holy Spirit within us—the Spirit who, according to Scripture, really dwells in us, lives in us, groans in us, cries in us, and intercedes in us. We can sadden the Spirit, extinguish the Spirit within us, by this or that way of acting. But we are unaware or almost unaware of him because our hearts are asleep. There is a saying of Abba Pambo that is all the more pointed for its brevity: "Acquire a heart and you can be saved." "Acquire a heart": this implies that we do not yet have that spiritual sensitivity—that alertness of heart—that can discern and understand the things of the Spirit. We must realize that not only is the Spirit given to us but he is also extending himself in us: the Spirit is essentially growth. A seed has been sown in our hearts which is a principle of life. It is the breath of God, but it also spreads in us, invades us, besieges us, and occupies us entirely—body, heart, and mind, judging our faith, our methods, our techniques, our conduct, and our activities.

We also have a number of interior senses that must be awakened and made sensitive to the activity of the Holy Spirit, senses that become sharper as our spiritual experience progresses. "Truly, anyone who is still living on milk," says the author of the Letter to the Hebrews, "cannot *taste* the doctrine of righteousness because he is still a baby. Solid food is for the mature whose minds are trained by practice to distinguish between good and bad" (5:14). The word translated as "minds" is in Greek *aisthêtêria*: it is the inner sensitivity, the deep connaturality with the things of the Spirit, for which we—or at least the mature[1]—have been trained by practice so that we may know how to discern good from evil. A little further on, that same letter speaks of those "who were once brought into the light and *tasted* the gift of heaven and received a share of the Holy Spirit and *savored* the good message of God and the powers of the world to come" (6:4).

---

[1] The "mature" are those who have been brought to their completion in Christ, as Christ was brought to his completion by his obedience and passion. They are those who have shared in the mystery of Christ in a closer, more urgent way.

Dwelling very briefly on a few points, I should now like to suggest: first, what could be called the subjective locus or organ of the Spirit in us; second, those places where the Spirit is objectively present; third and last, the activities of the Spirit.

The Subjective Place of the Spirit

Our organ for receiving the Spirit, which is the creative breath of God, is our whole self, body and soul—or body and heart, if you like. Note that the body is included. It does not disappear in the process of spiritualization. It simply passes from its "psychic" state, as Saint Paul calls it (its animal or fleshly state), into a spiritual state. For spiritual bodies do exist.

Everything that happens to the body happens through the Spirit. Saint Paul's respect for the body, with the strong link he sees between it and the Holy Spirit, is remarkable. The body is the temple of the Spirit, and it is by the Spirit that we mortify our members that are on the earth. Thus asceticism is something spiritual, the work of the Holy Spirit in us, bearing his mark. In asceticism, the Spirit cleaves, in a way, to the flesh and is incarnated in it, and the flesh adheres to the Spirit. Today, thank God, we have a number of techniques of inner asceticism and bodily asceticism, mental or spiritual hygiene, and bodily hygiene. They can be made to serve the life of the Spirit in us, but only, it seems to me, on condition that somewhere in the technique the Spirit intervenes to take over our human activity and make it fully fruitful. Only God, in the strength of the Spirit, can begin and perfect within us this process of the *Pasch*, of passing-over into the Spirit. Asceticism is a sign and miracle of the Holy Spirit, and if it is not—if it is not something within us yet beyond what we could do of ourselves, humanly speaking—then it is not yet Christian asceticism. In the last analysis, all asceticism of the body (as in the case of celibacy for Saint Paul) is a matter of adhering to the Lord through our bodies, becoming one Spirit with him in our bodies.

But it is above all the heart that is the true dwelling place of the Holy Spirit. It is there that "the Spirit bears witness to our spirit that we are children of God." It is the heart that listens, consents, is impregnated, assimilates the Spirit as it assimilates the Word, and bears its fruit of praise and Eucharist.

The Objective Places of the Spirit

We must now say something about the "places" outside of us where we experience the Spirit, where the grace of the *Pasch* wells up ceaselessly and is, so to speak, at our disposal.

The first is the Word of God, of which Isaiah says comes from God and does not return to him without having borne fruit in the world and in us. Now the Word of God is sown in the heart, and this impact of the Word on us is "original" in the strongest sense of the word. Our heart awakens; our whole personality assumes its full stature and finds its identity. For the heart is the specific organ for God's Word: the Word is made for the heart, and the heart is made for the Word. It follows that we can only fully grasp the Word of God in our hearts. The Word can stray into our minds or into our imaginations and superficial affectivities, but then its properly divine and creative strength becomes weakened. The Word is the two-edged sword of which the Letter to the Hebrews speaks (4:12), which alone can reach the depths of man's heart, lay it bare and reveal it to him. So much so that Saint Peter, in his first letter (1 Pet 1:23), can speak of our being born of God's Word. We are begotten anew by the Word as by an incorruptible seed, and only the fruit of this Word within us is destined to survive the flesh.

Another locus of the Spirit for us, and one which we would do well to explore, is the Name of God—concretely, the Name of JESUS—in whom is revealed to us all the fullness of the Godhead. This name situates us both in the world and before God. We are brought together in this Name, and people hate us because of it. Our foreheads and our hearts are marked with the Name of the Lamb: this is the mysterious sign of which Ezekiel speaks, the letter *Tau* of the Aramaic alphabet, which in the time of Jesus was written in the form of a cross and which Christians from the Judeo-Christian period onward have interpreted as a symbol of the cross and resurrection.

Another locus where we experience the Spirit, and where the Spirit tests us, is the will of God, or more precisely, the will of the Father: "Thy will be done on earth as it is in heaven." The Father's will is God's desire, God's joy, God's good pleasure. It coincides with the most intimate and secret depths of our being, but unfortunately we really become aware of it only when we want to go against it. For we come up against this will of God, or rather, with our small passions and self-will we set ourselves in opposition to the great desire of God urging us to the fulfillment of his mystery.

Another locus we could discuss is communion, *koinônia*: the communion in the Body of Christ, which is the Church and which is slowly and surely being gathered together in the Holy Spirit and all that this communion represents in the way of sharing, of proclamation of the Word, of service to our brothers and sisters, and, above all, of gratuitous love: "We know that we have passed from death to life because we love our brothers and sisters" (1 John 3:14).

Yet another locus of the Spirit is the desert. The desert was the place of the People of God, the place where Jesus was driven by the Spirit when he withdrew into solitude. It is also the place where the Church is called by the Spirit today, like the woman of the Apocalypse who was withdrawn into the desert just when persecution was becoming most violent. I am not speaking here primarily of the monastic desert but of the Christian desert. The monastic desert is usually a physical desert; but the monk lives his life in it as a sacrament of the monastic aspect of the Church, a special sacrament in which he expresses his own vocation, for such is the grace he has received. But the Church herself is always and wholly in the desert; she is in a diaspora situation, especially today. We find ourselves thrown back by all the questions which are put to us and to which we can find no immediate answer— thrown back into an inner desert. But this is at the same time an invitation to greater depth in the poverty of our comprehension, for we are reduced to the witness of the Spirit alone, speaking within us, and we are not to think beforehand what to say.

The desert evokes another locus of the Spirit: temptation. Not our small daily temptations, but *the* unique temptation, the great eschatological temptation, that of the last days in which we are already living. We must recognize this temptation in everything that happens to us, as in the contrarieties and sufferings around us. "Consider it all joy, my brothers and sisters, when you encounter various trials," says Saint James at the beginning of his letter, "for you know that the testing of your faith produces perseverance" (1:2-3). It is in the moment of trial or temptation that the witness of the Spirit becomes clear and eloquent within us, and it is in the very thick of temptation that Christians recognize each other as brothers and sisters. Temptation places us before God in an altogether new way. It is an open breach in us. Every temptation questions a certain number of structures—not only structures of the Church but also the structures of our own inner personality, too. Because it disconcerts and unseats us, because it opens a breach and dismantles something within us, temptation brings with it the possibility of a rich outpouring of grace and of growth in the Holy Spirit. If we can bring ourselves to accept this dismantling and to appear in all our weakness and poverty, these will very soon be replaced and taken over by the power of God which works to the full in our weakness. This acceptance is essentially what *hypomonê*, patience, is.

Finally, there is a locus of the Spirit about which I will be very brief because it is one of which we have no direct experience. It is very important, perhaps the most important of all. I mean *death*, in which everything is given to us at once, like a ripe fruit waiting at the end of a long initiation, a long training. Here, if we ourselves cannot bear witness to the Spirit's activity, it would perhaps be interesting to study and analyze the testimonies of the dying. Perhaps it is in them that we shall discover the true criteria for experience of the Spirit.

The Activities of the Spirit

Again briefly, I should like to enumerate some activities of the Spirit within us. I use the word "activity" not with the meaning we usually give it but in the biblical sense of *energeia*, the "energies" of the Spirit within us, or *dynamis*, "power," the dynamism of the Spirit within us. The first activity or energy of the Spirit within us is *metanoia*, repentance. This turning back of our *nous* (*meta-noia*), this change of heart, is our first moment of truth before God, before ourselves, and before our brothers and sisters. Some fathers of the Church held that it normally implies the baptism of tears, which for them is the sign that the Holy Spirit is besieging a person's body: the person capitulates, his resistance gives way, and he weeps. Parallels could be drawn here with experiences that occur in psychoanalysis: there is a kind of *catharsis*. The man weeps and surrenders, surrenders to the Holy Spirit, to that new awareness of himself that he acquires in the baptism of tears. I realize that repentance is not only a difficult theme to touch on today but also is—given the complexes of our times—one of the most difficult to pin down and to live out authentically. And yet it remains essential. In general, repentance is refused today. We live at the turning point between the obsessive neurosis (if I may call it that) characterizing the generation just before ours and the adolescent effervescence and aggressiveness of a generation that is now freeing itself from this neurosis. Proof that he has sinned can only create unbearable anguish in one who is already eaten up with anguish. Sin was intolerable for the period immediately before our own, and people tried to free themselves from it by what the fathers called *dikaioma*, the pretension of justice. Sin is unbearable, so one claims to be just by an outward observance of law, or rather, of a certain number of regulations; in reality, one is fleeing from *metanoia*. Today, instead, we have an adolescent effervescence and aggressiveness which are just as unbearable. The solution now, however, is to say that there is no such thing as sin.

Another energy of the Spirit, one bound up with compunction, is *birth*. We must be born of the Spirit, says Scripture, born of the will of God which is love, born of the Word, born again. This is an experience of the Holy Spirit. Here would be the place to speak of faith, which is essentially a seeing in the Spirit, and of discernment, which is very difficult indeed, so difficult that in almost all his letters Saint Paul prays for those he is writing to, asking God to reveal his will fully to them.

Another activity of the Spirit within us is *looking*. Looking gradually prepares us for seeing. "The world will not see me, but you shall see me, because I live, and you shall live" (John 14:19). We see the Lord not according to the flesh, which is impossible, but with vision in the Holy Spirit. We recognize Christ in things, in faces, and finally in the icon, the inner vision, that we carry in our heart.

Yet another energy of the Spirit in us is *agapê*. This is love as the sign that we have met God and have been forgiven by him. We are the reproduction, the extension of the *agapê* of God, which has overflowed in our hearts and which we can now share with our brothers and sisters. Here we may ask ourselves the question: To what extent do we first have to experience the *agapê* of God before we can share it with others? And to what extent must we try first of all to love others in order to discover, through this still imperfect, hesitant, and shaky love, the *agapê* of God? Though these two ways are different, no doubt they are both ways of the Spirit.

Then there is that energy of the Spirit that is *lowliness*. I do not use the word "humility" here because the usual meaning we give it implies self-assessment, which is something that only comes, I feel, as an afterthought. Humility is a condition before it is self-judgment. It is a lowly condition drawing on the example of Christ: "He who humbles himself will be exalted" (Luke 14:11). This lowliness is of value only if it comes from the Holy Spirit. Here no doubt is where religious obedience comes in, insofar as it is a situation of submission, of subjection to others, practiced out of love for the Lord and in imitation of him.

Again, there is the energy of the Spirit that is *combat*—combat engaged in with the sword of the Spirit and the strength of the glory of God. Within this combat is situated the preeminent Christian virtue, which is patience. This admirable *hypomônê* has nothing in common with Stoicism or with specifically pagan attitudes or forms of endurance. "May you be made strong with all the strength that comes from his glorious power, and may you be prepared to endure everything with patience!" (Col 1:11). This strength of God, which is the strength of the Spirit, is the particular characteristic of the Christian. One who depends wholly on the Word will bear the fruit of the Word in *hypomônê*, as Saint Luke says (8:15). He holds the Word and (in the strongest sense) keeps it. He clings to the Word against all hope and beyond all hope, stretching forward in expectation, torn by his desire and yet already borne up by a great confidence. All this is contained in a saying which almost certainly comes from Jesus himself: *In patientia vestra possidebitis animas vestras*—literally, "In your patience you shall possess your souls" (Luke 21:19). In Greek and Latin this is a rather enigmatic phrase. If we try to change it back into the original Aramaic, however, I think we get the following meaning: "In patience you will take on your true faces, you will be fully yourselves." One's true Christian personality is realized in patience.

Finally, the last energy of the Spirit within us, the double fruit of the Spirit, is *witness and proclamation*, on the one hand, and *prayer* on the other. This is certainly a double energy, and we may not separate one part from the other. Both modalities of this energy of the Spirit are possible, both are of equal value, and both are one, for they are the fruit of the Word within us when it has truly come to maturity in our hearts and is proclaimed by the Spirit within us. It is interesting that, in his *Life of Saint Antony*, Saint Athanasius speaks of Antony's double martyrdom. He means first the witness given by Saint Antony against the Arians at Alexandria, proclaiming the Word by his presence, and secondly, prayer, which he calls the "martyrdom of consciousness." Prayer is martyrdom in the sense of "witness," and consciousness is the organ of prayer, that is to say, the heart, the inner person. The Christian who has acquired her full stature in Christ is both a witness and a person of prayer. She witnesses and prays continually in the Spirit—that Spirit who finally becomes our prayer, in the measure in which his own prayer, his own cry, emerges from our unconscious and is assimilated by our heart.

2

The Contemplative Life

Fifty years of *aggiornamento* have permitted monks to arrive at a better understanding of their contemplative life and to make it more intelligible to others. The exterior framework has been transformed: observances have been simplified, the rhythm has been made more peaceful, the whole of the life finds itself returned to tasting the One Thing Necessary.

The most important change, however, has taken place within hearts. If the contemplative rejoices always at having received the call—however unworthy of it he may be—to what is conventionally called "the better part," he henceforth situates this vocation differently. He is less than ever tempted to push his way to the forefront of the Church, to the premiere ranks, so to speak. He has rediscovered his true place, that of the publican in the gospel, at the farthest back, and he takes up the invocation—"Have pity on me, a sinner!"—that Saint Benedict confided to him as the perfect and perpetual formula of prayer. A deepened experience of his contemplative calling has taught him this. In what does this experience consist?

At the back of the Church, I was saying, and yet always at the heart of the Church, and now more than ever. The contemplative must, first of all, be where the Church finds herself, like the Hebrew people at the Exodus and where her master, Jesus, found himself during his fast: that is, perpetually in the desert, in the place of her origins, where God calls her "to speak to her heart . . . and to espouse her forever" (Hos 2:14). In her contemplatives, the Church listens unceasingly to the Word and is daily reborn of it and, though she is turned toward the world and fully engaged in it, she finds herself at the same time immersed in the desert. This dialogue of love between her and her Spouse, to which certain people are exclusively vowed, can alone assure her of the authenticity of her message.

Again, assiduous listening to the Word of God, in the liturgy celebrated in common or in that private liturgy that is *lectio divina*, becomes the principal occupation of the contemplative, the source from which he nourishes his prayer. The Word that is listened to, lovingly meditated on, and patiently assimilated, finally gushes forth in thanksgiving, in praise, and in intercession, sometimes also in sharing with someone who comes to ask for a word. The contemplative is the Word become prayer.

The way is long, for this life in the desert and this exodus do not consist only in repose. Like Jesus, the contemplative has been led into the desert to be tempted by the devil. There is no other door of entry into Christian contemplation, and it is particularly narrow. The first trial comes to the contemplative from that very environment—the desert—which he has generously chosen, believing to find there the sure path toward his goal, to learn the diverse forms of what has traditionally been called asceticism: fasting, vigils, solitude, silence.

These ascetical practices exist in many other religions. Nonetheless, one should make no mistake here: in the light of the gospel and in the person of Jesus, the meaning of these practices is completely altered. They no longer facilitate anything, much less do they merit what can be nothing but the absolutely gratuitous gift of Love. They henceforth serve one sole purpose—what one least expected: to plunge ever more deeply into the abyss of one's total poverty before the divine offer. For from being an occasion for showing one's prowess in generosity, Christian asceticism is meant to become a place of defeat where the grace of God alone triumphs inasmuch as it demonstrates one's radical weakness wherein the power of grace can be at last unleashed. The contemplative comes to experience very concretely the extent to which all his good works are simply miracles of grace.

No way is more sorrowful than this, nor arrives at a submission to so radical a stripping—that of evangelical humility. Many contemplatives stop midway, reckoning that their supposed virtue is incompatible with such abasement in their own eyes, sometimes even in the eyes of others. There is nevertheless no way but this one, where the contemplative learns that he is not better than his brothers, that he is a sinner forgiven for as much and even more than they, and that, in order to advance more than his brothers in contemplation, he must join those to whom Jesus has promised precedence in his kingdom. He thus becomes the Church of humble and joyous repentance.

It is a humility all the more radical in that it reaches the contemplative even in that very desire that constitutes the heart of his vocation: the desire of seeing and knowing a God who seems to hide himself in incurable weakness, who constantly denudes himself unto such a poverty. This God appears so far off and even, at certain moments, as if "dead," inexistent, a mirage, a projection into infinity of one's own desires. Hence the contemplative finds himself at the heart of his desert, or in the dark night, even in the mystery of Jesus himself crying out: "My God, my God, why have you abandoned me?!" (Matt 27:46). The night may perhaps be brief, or it may be prolonged, apparently endless, according to the good pleasure of God's grace and to the measure of each individual vocation. More than other believers, the contemplative ought to be an "expert in atheism." Does he believe? Perhaps, yet without believing, it seems to him. He no longer understands anything except this one thing: that the God in whom he thought he believed is nothing but an idol invented by himself or fashioned by a culture still vaguely imprinted by Christianity; that the true God, the God of Jesus Christ, is a wholly Other who will surge forth elsewhere than where one expected him, and that one must above all abandon the attempt to reach him by one's own efforts. And yet it suffices to let him remain unattainable and to let oneself by seized by him at the hour of his own good pleasure.

It is in this underground of humility, as Ruysbroeck called it, that the miracle can take place in which God becomes "sensible to the heart," that one can "taste how good is the Lord." More than ever, the contemplative thus becomes the Church that somehow hastens on the joys of heaven. "But it is in the night" that this occurs, as John of the Cross said or, rather, from night to night, and from glow of dawn to glow of dawn culled, so to speak, from the Word of God, a lamp for one's steps, and illumined by it as by the morning star, until the risen sun comes to inundate with its light the Church in her entirety.

From this spiritual adventure, there remains one more element to indicate, and not the least one, since I speak here in the name of families of religious. It is germane to a community of brothers, a community that is therefore of necessity both school of humility and way of contemplation: how can one claim to truly love God without also loving one's brothers? As a *Schola caritatis*, school of humble love and school of contemplation, the contemplative community gives itself to become, if God wills, a micro-Church that God has chosen for himself and offered to himself, in order that there may already be celebrated here and now the wedding feast between his Son and the Bride whom he has redeemed and whom he offers to the world, that she may become a foretaste of what will be our common joy for endless ages.

In conclusion, it remains for me to suggest some convergences between the contemplative life as understood in the foregoing and certain appeals addressed to the Church today.

Simply in being itself, without claiming anything more, the contemplative life can reawaken, in the believer as well as the unbeliever, the desire for communion with God that lies dormant in the human heart. Purified of his false gods, the contemplative feels close to all those who doubt and search, particularly to those who believe themselves to be atheists. He is especially close to sinners in danger of despair, who frequently come knocking at his door because he offers some experience of the overwhelming mercy of God and because he knows well that joyful repentance is the only way of knowing how much we are loved, and this equally for the sinner and for the just person.

The contemplative life witnesses to an authentically evangelical "technique," if you will pardon the expression, in the service of contemplation, which must be known and lived for its own sake before dialogue can usefully be engaged with other non-Christian techniques.

The contemplative life is a marvelous school of discernment where, in the course of the contemplative adventure, one learns to recognize the true consolations of the Spirit among so many desires swarming in the heart. It is thus a possible locus of dialogue between the spiritual tradition of the Church and certain attainments of the human sciences.

Finally, the contemplative life is par excellence a context for ecumenism in which the God-seekers of Christian traditions of both East and West can meet and, going beyond theological barriers, foster communion not only with each other but also equally with the God-seekers and the mystics of non-Christian religions.

I end by citing two modern sayings. An Orthodox monk visiting a Trappist house confessed to having discovered there "a corner of Orthodoxy in the Latin Church." And better still: a young Muslim, recently finding himself in another Trappist monastery, exclaimed: "I have finally found some true Muslims!"

3

The Common Life: A School of Charity

The sight of brothers or sisters celebrating the liturgy together, praying and working in common but also in silence, living under the same roof and withdrawn from the world: this is the image that has been the point of departure for many Cistercian vocations. In such a community, many of us recognized the answer to the yearning of our hearts and therefore decided to join. Indeed, we would have been able to cry out, with William of Saint-Thierry perceiving Clairvaux from far off nestled in its valley: "In this valley filled with men, well-ordered love has made a solitary place for each brother, thanks to the discipline of the Order. For [the Order] defended the solitude of the heart of each brother, in the very bosom of a well-ordered multitude, thanks to the unity of spirit of all and thanks to the law of regular silence."[1]

In fact, such a choice was not ours to make. Rather, what Saint Luke noted regarding the first Christians came to be realized again in our lives: "Every day the Lord added to the community those who were to find salvation" (Acts 2:47). We really did not have to choose. We had been chosen. Nor, indeed, had we been chosen by the members of this community that did not know us, but rather by the Lord himself who had made the choice of this community for us and of us for the community. Given to each other by the free gift of the Lord, it is henceforth through this gift

---

[1] William of Saint-Thierry, *Life of Saint Bernard* 7.36.

15

and the beginning of communion that it establishes that we must wait for, and hasten on to, our meeting with him.[2]

Just as the gift was unexpected and gratuitous, so also will the path be disconcerting, but its fruit will be beyond anything we would have dared to hope for: a long and patient apprenticeship in the gratuitousness of love. It is this more particular, and necessarily limited, aspect—the pedagogy of the Cistercian life as a "school of love"[3]—that I will here seek to bring to light.[4]

Socialis gratiae suavitas: The Sweetness and the Grace of Being Together[5]

However reasonable the choice of our way of life may have seemed at its commencement, its deepest motives escaped us. Many are the motives that could have led us to prefer such a life to more solitary, and perhaps more risky, forms of monastic life: the "consolations afforded by companions on the way,"[6] the assurance of being helped in case of difficulty,[7] the edifying example of the brothers. Like the young Antony before he retired definitively from the commerce of his brothers, we had the impression that we could locate in each of the brothers some

---

[2] *Nam et disciplina et socialis vita donum gratiae est*: Bernard of Clairvaux, *Diverse Sermons* 92.2 (hereafter *Div.*), in *Sermons divers*, introduction and notes by P.-Y. Émery (Paris: Desclée de Brouwer, 1982).

[3] *Specialis caritatis schola*, in William of Saint-Thierry, *On the Nature and Dignity of Love* 9.26 (hereafter *NatDigAm*), seems to present the most ancient usage; *Schola dilectionis*, in Bernard of Clairvaux, *Div.* 121; *schola pietatis*, again in Bernard of Clairvaux, *Sermons on the Canticle of Canticles* 69.2 (hereafter *CC*).

[4] Several recent works have inspired this document: B. Olivera, "Aspectos del amor al prójimo en la doctrina espiritual de San Bernardo," *Analecta Cisterciensia* 46 (1990): 151–97; M. Casey, "*In communi vita fratrum*: Saint Bernard's teaching on cenobitic solitude," *Analecta Cisterciensia* 46 (1990): 243–61; T. Davis, "Cistercian *Communio*," *Cistercian Studies* 29 (1994): 291–329; G. Raciti, "L'option préférentielle pour les faibles dans le modèle communautaire aelrédien," *Collectanea Cisterciensia* 55 (1993): 186–206.

[5] The expression *socialis gratiae suavitas* is from Bernard of Clairvaux, *CC* 44.5.

[6] *Conviatorum solatia*, in: Bernard of Clairvaux, *Sentences* 2.76 (hereafter *Sent.*).

[7] Saint Bernard often repeats the admonition of Ecclesiastes 4:10: "Woe to the solitary man, for he has no one to pick him up when he falls."

particular grace that could nourish our hopes and our efforts: "Antony considered the good humor of one and the assiduity at prayer of another; he observed the sweetness of spirit of this one and the kindness of that one; he noted the vigils of one and the love of *lectio* of another; he admired the patience of some and the fasts and austerities of others . . . ; but above all, he inscribed in his heart the love they all had for Jesus Christ and the charity they bore toward one another."[8]

Who, then, has not sought to experience something of the "paradise of the cloister," as Saint Bernard called it,[9] or even of the "celestial paradise" that William caught a glimpse of, as he depicts it in a colorful description of the cenobitic community?[10] The same Bernard puts us on guard, however: what one learns and lives as a young candidate is but a modest debut: "It is a flower, the time for fruit has not yet arrived."[11] It is a hope of fruit, well-founded to the extent that the novice has already established a link between his attraction for God and this fraternal life, even if this life has not yet revealed all of its exigencies.

If, however, he is sufficiently experienced, he will guess rather quickly that the initial joys, indeed even the enthusiasm that the fraternal life inspires in him, are marked by a certain ambiguity. If he identifies himself easily with the community, it is also because it corresponds—without his being conscious of the fact—to his own self-image, an image still highly idealized and more than flattering. If he has not yet reached the height of the community, this height nevertheless represents for him the height of what he secretly wants to become. Without knowing it, he has annexed the community to a narcissistic image of himself. From this stems his desire that it be as perfect as possible, without spot or wrinkle—in short, worthy of him—as well as the irritation that overwhelms him each time reality comes to threaten his expectations. He is

---

[8] Athanasius, *Life of Antony*, 2, SC 400 (Paris: Éditions du Cerf, 1994).

[9] Cf. *Div*. 42:4, where Bernard develops a "Cistercian" version of the host of virtues offered to the candidate in the *Life of Antony*. Cf. equally *CC* 63.6.

[10] Cf. William of Saint-Thierry, *NatDignAm* 24–27.

[11] Cf. Bernard of Clairvaux, *CC* 63.6.

not yet a true man of the community but rather a solitary who does not know himself,[12] who makes use of others for so long as they flatter his self-image but who rejects them brutally, even condemns them, from the moment they call him into question. The first stage, however fecund, will be one day surpassed. The wear and tear of time and fraternal life will make sure of it, at the hour appointed by God.

Labor humilitatis: The Labor of Humility[13]

At several places in his writings, Saint John Cassian weighs carefully the respective advantages and disadvantages of the solitary and the common life. According to Cassian, the common life precedes the solitary life not only in time but also in grace.[14] Among other advantages, it possesses that of bringing into the light of day the weakness and the sin of the monk, whereas solitude temporarily conceals them and thus opens the way to illusion. It is impossible to live among brothers without their presence revealing our faults: if we withdraw into the desert without having first been healed of our vices, we not only hinder their fruits, but the root of sin remains hidden in our heart. Far from having been extinguished, the passion grows secretly.[15] Now, it is important to know one's sin in order to be moved to repentance, for only repentance can heal us.[16]

Thus fraternal life rather quickly presents itself as a mirror, however irritating, of our own imperfections. At that juncture, we are far removed from our cenobitic first fervor. In this connection, Cassian's testimony is corroborated by Bernard, who describes this process in detail in the *Treatise on the Love of God* and in the

---

[12] Cf. Bernard of Clairvaux, *The Degrees of Humility and Pride* 17 (hereafter *GradHum*). The Pharisee, says Bernard, gives thanks to God not for being a good man but rather for being the only good man (*non quia bonus, sed quia solus bonus*).

[13] The expression, "labor of humility" is from Bernard of Clairvaux, *GradHum* 6.19.

[14] *Antiquissimum monachorum genus, quod non solum tempore, set etiam gratia primum est.* John Cassian, *Conferences* 18.5.

[15] *Conferences* 19.12.

[16] *Conferences* 19.16.

Degrees of Humility and Pride. The first step is the recognition of one's own misery which brushes up against discouragement, a misery that only becomes a source of salvation when "from justice it takes refuge in mercy."[17]

Bernard considers this step decisive: the *labor humilitatis*,[18] the labor or ascesis of humility. At once psychological and spiritual, this work is of the first importance. Today, one would call it the acceptance of oneself, along with one's past, one's memories, one's inevitable frustrations, and one's limits. Such a work can be begun only under the enlightened and benevolent gaze of a spiritual companion. It will not reach its true completion until it meets the merciful gaze of God. Since God loves us just as we are, why should not we in turn love ourselves as we are, without false shame, without neurotic feelings of guilt? This is why, as surprising as it may seem, the first degree of the love of others and of God is, for Bernard, the merciful love of oneself.

In this training in self-acceptance, the community plays an important role. First, our brothers show us our poverty. The tempests of aggression, rivalry, and jealousy that they unwittingly release in us put our poor resources to the test. Of course, it is a good tactic to learn to be content in the face of these storms, but that is not enough. They have another fruit to bear: they warrant interpretation because whatever irritates us in our brothers teaches us first of all something about ourselves. It is our own scars that begin to bleed again, our own weaknesses that feel threatened. This is not to say that the irritation we experience has no objective cause in this or that fault of a brother, but only that any inopportune intervention on our part, in his regard, would be inefficacious as long as we are not reconciled with the wound within us. Saint Benedict knew this when he required of spiritual fathers that they know how to heal their own wounds at the same time that they heal those of the brothers.[19]

---

[17] See Bernard of Clairvaux, *GradHum* 5.18.
[18] *GradHum* 6.19.
[19] See *Rule of Saint Benedict* 46.6 (hereafter RB).

This *labor humilitatis* constitutes a decisive step in the monastic journey. Its fruit will be what the tradition calls *contritio cordis* or "breaking of the heart," using an image borrowed from Psalm 50:19: "You do not spurn a crushed and broken heart." In what does this breaking consist? It takes place in the heart, harassed and as it were exhausted by temptations, humiliated and at the point of discouragement in view of its incorrigible weakness, and at length laying down the arms with which it had unconsciously struggled against grace, and finally consenting to deliver itself in its present state to the gentle mercy of the Savior. Its resistance is now broken, its pride crushed. The true "me" can come into the light of day under the kindly gaze of God, most often in an outpouring of very sweet tears, those of repentance, a second baptism.[20] We are here at the heart of the Gospel and of the Christian and monastic experience. The joy is very great. Under the pen of Benedict it becomes the "inexpressible sweetness of love."[21]

But before arriving there, the crisis must be prolonged, sometimes for a man's entire lifetime, or nearly so. Within a common life, it is the brotherhood itself that becomes the privileged theater and instrument of this crisis. Saint Benedict describes its elements and its stakes in the fourth degree of humility. This degree has been called the "night" of the cenobite. As a matter of fact, it is the cenobitic framework itself that becomes the supreme temptation. It lacks nothing in Benedict's description: neither situations of injustice, nor the contrary superior, nor false brothers. In addition, there is the "snare," the "fire of the crucible," the "slaughterhouse" and "death." One has no choice but to abandon oneself to the love of the Lord: "But in all this we are more than conquerors because of him who has loved us."[22]

---

[20] Bernard describes how to "cooperate" in this breaking of the heart with a "feeling of gentle mercy" for oneself, which makes of humility a veritable *curatio* (cure), see *Div.* 20.5.

[21] See RB Prol. 49.

[22] See RB 7. For the ancient monastic tradition, not only the common life of the cenobite but also the solitude of the hermit, as well as different practices of classical asceticism (vigils, fasting, sleeping on hard surfaces), all had the same objective: the breaking of the heart, that is to say, bringing the monk to despair

Affectus compassionis: **The Heart Touched by Compassion**[23]

It is in loving oneself with a merciful love, the same love that one has experienced on the part of God at the heart of the crisis, that one begins to love one's brothers. From the experience of one's own sufferings, one comes to feel compassion for those of others.[24] And this knowledge of compassion opens a way of access to contemplation. Bernard notes that, in the gospel, the beatitude of mercy precedes that of the pure of heart who see God, because the heart needs to be purified by mercy before it can be capable of contemplation. Now, "to have a heart that is merciful toward the misery of others, it is first of all necessary to have recognized one's own misery."[25]

The sweet sharing of the common life thus reveals itself first of all in the sharing of the common misery: "Aware of our common weakness, we must humble ourselves, each one before the other, and mutually embrace each other in pity, so that the proud exaltation of certain ones may not divide those who are rendered equal by the same condition of weakness," writes Baldwin of Ford in a celebrated little treatise dedicated to our theme.[26] The climate of the Cistercian common life is thus pregnant with authentic evangelical graces, namely, according to the same author, "Mutual patience, mutual humility, mutual charity."[27] For the sight and the acceptance of the common misery demand a common mercy.

---

of himself so that he may put all his confidence in God alone. "A brother asked: 'What is accomplished by the fasts and vigils that a man practices?' The elder replied: 'Their effect is to humble the heart. For it is written: *See my lowliness and my toil and pardon all my sins.* If someone thus practices ascesis, God will take pity on him'" (*Vita Patrum*, 6.4.5; see *Sayings of the Desert Fathers*, "Moses," 18b [hereafter *Sayings*]). In this connection, see the famous *Letter of Saint Macarius to His Sons*, trans. André Louf, in *Lettres des Pères du désert*, coll. *Spiritualité orientale* 42 (Bégrolles-en-Mauges: Éditions de Bellefontaine, 1985).

[23] The expression *affectus compassionis* is of Bernard of Clairvaux (*GradHum* 6.19).

[24] *Dum ex his quae patiuntur, patientibus compati sciunt* (*GradHum* 5.18).

[25] *GradHum* 3.6.

[26] Baldwin of Ford, *On the Common Life*, PL 204, 551 C.

[27] *On the Common Life*, 558–59.

Communal Therapy

In such a climate, fraternal life can assume the power of psychological and spiritual healing that transform the common life into a veritable course of therapy. For Saint Bernard, the "balm of mercy" is "an ointment."[28] His Second Sermon for Easter describes the steps and the conditions of this treatment. Even today, he claims, mercy joined to "patience with a humble affection"[29] can raise to life a brother who lies dead in his tomb. The merciful brother thus recovers a quality natural to the human person when sin had not yet obscured it: "A sort of fluidity of an extreme and very pleasant gentleness that renders him tender so that he might have compassion on sinners, rather than bitter so that he becomes indignant at them."[30] Saint Benedict thus recommends that the abbot "always prefer mercy to justice, so as one day to be treated in the same manner."[31] Equally for Bernard, mercy becomes irresistible to such a point that he avows that even if, by an impossibility, it were a sin, he could not restrain himself from committing it.[32] And the unforgettable accent with which he was often obliged to comment on mercy in his chapter talks is condensed in a bold affirmation that he borrows from the *Exordium Magnum*, namely, that even Judas—had he become a monk at Clairvaux—would have found salvation.[33]

If sin and forgiveness form part of the monastic itinerary, it is normal for the weak and for sinners to find a place in the community. They are awaited there. A community that excluded sinners would cease to be Christian. For where sin is denied to

---

[28] *Unguentum pietatis* [. . .] *sanativum est* (Bernard of Clairvaux, CC 12.1). Cf. Bernard of Clairvaux, *Sermons for the Annunciation* 3.1 (hereafter *Ann.*): "Is not mercy a food for human beings? Yes, a salutary food whose power gives healing."

[29] *Patientia in pietate* (Bernard of Clairvaux, *Second Sermon for Easter*, 11, trans. P.-Y. Émery, in Bernard of Clairvaux, *Sermons pour l'année* [Taizé: Brepols, 1990], 492).

[30] *Gratae et egregiae quasi suavitatis liquor* (Bernard of Clairvaux, CC 44.4). The Curé of Ars uses the same image in speaking of the "liquid heart of the saints."

[31] See RB 64.10.

[32] See Bernard of Clairvaux, Letter 70.

[33] See *Exordium Magnum Cisterciense* 2.5.

that extent, or rather ingeniously disguised, grace no longer has any place and God is deprived of his greatest joy, which is to welcome a sinner who repents. We would be in another world, the world of the "righteous," as the gospel calls them, the "righteous" who have no need of repentance (Luke 15:7): in short, the world of the Pharisees.[34]

Contrariwise, through mercy both the weakest and the strongest can breathe in the same atmosphere, that of God himself, because no one bears a stronger resemblance to God than one who is merciful to his brothers. In the case of an Aelred, for example, one could speak of a veritable "preferential option for the poor" within his abbey.[35] His biographer does not hesitate to call the monastery of Rievaulx the "Mother of Mercy," so numerous were those who "from foreign lands and from vast distances, having need of fraternal mercy, came there seeking refuge."[36]

"Having need of fraternal mercy": these words recall those we monks pronounced, lying prostrate before the community when we were being admitted: "What do you seek?" "The mercy of God and of the Order." We needed this double mercy in order to be reconciled with ourselves and to discover, behind the face of "fraternal mercy," the face of the true God. This is especially the ministry of the abbot, but it would scarcely be efficacious if the brothers did not share in it in one way or another. Bernard knew such brothers: "Devout, affectionate, agreeable, supple, humble, they not only endure patiently the infirmities of bodies and souls

---

[34] The apparent severity of Saint Benedict who, in certain cases, does not hesitate to "excommunicate" a brother, should not be misconstrued. It forms part of a therapeutic process and does not come into play until all other means have been exhausted. But above all, the goal of this is the healing of the brother "that his spirit may be saved on the day of judgment." Besides, it suffices to turn one's attention to the rite of reconciliation—greatly detailed in the Rule of the Master and clearly presupposed by Benedict—to convince oneself that the suffering imposed by the excommunication is entirely for the sake of the joy of a return to the sheepfold. See RB 24–28.

[35] See Raciti, "L'option préférentielle pour les faibles dans le modèle communitaire aelrédien," 186–206.

[36] See Walter Daniel, *Vita Ailredi Abbatis Rievallensis*, ed. and trans. Maurice Powicke (Oxford, UK: Clarendon Press, 1950), section 29.

but they also help their brothers by their service, comfort them by their words, instruct them by their counsels, and, if the rule of silence does not permit [these beneficial words], they at least do not cease to support the weak brother by ardent prayers. . . . Such a brother in the community is like a balm in the mouth. Everyone points him out and says of him: 'Here is one who loves his brothers and the people Israel, who prays constantly for the people and for all the holy city.'"[37] Such monks and nuns can be found in every Cistercian community. They are its hidden treasure. They are therapists to their brothers, living icons of Christ the servant in the midst of those who are his, whose "humble love" builds up the Church.

Love and Observances

The mercy of the community engenders an evangelical way of living the observances. The latter are fundamental for monastic life. They give a particular face to the charism of the group and constitute the skeleton of the common life. Above all, they specify the concrete terrain where each one will exercise his own particular grace. In this sense, they must be an invitation for the strong and, at the same time, be a protection for the weak who, thanks to the observances, need never become discouraged.[38] The manner of living the observances, however, can vary considerably from one epoch to another, from one culture to another, from one age to another. A certain rigor imposed on the whole community, the ambiguous and illusory ideal of a perfect regularity, can close the doors to love. Aelred employs severe expressions to, as it were, flog the bitter zeal of certain observant monks "who are puffed up with a false justice, despise all the others and refuse to place themselves on the level of the brothers out of any sense of compassion whatsoever. . . . Among such people, the strength

---

[37] See Bernard of Clairvaux, CC 12.5; cf. CC 12.1: an equally detailed description of the merciful monk.

[38] See RB 64: "That the strong may have something to strive for and the weak nothing to run from."

of love is not virtue but rather vice, they who despise others because they are able to keep vigil, to fast, and to pray more than the others."[39] The goal of asceticism obviously does not consist in this proud closing off of oneself. Quite the contrary, the goal lies precisely in the agonizing coming to awareness of one's misery, called the "breaking of the heart," shared fraternally with the others, so as to experience the same sweetness of mercy. Once again, it is Bernard who exhorts us not to flee the common misery so as remain in the mercy, because he who "hides his misery, chases away mercy."[40]

Such a way of living the observances presupposes a delicate equilibrium between their clear and intelligible presentation by the superior and the "merciful" way of administering them in the concrete situations of life or, in other words, the balance between the Rule and what Bernard called "dispensation"—the manner of applying the Rule to the concrete situations of life.[41] This equilibrium presumes a continual discernment on the part of those holding responsibility and of the spiritual fathers, so that the traditional pedagogy of observances and the necessary fraternal correction that accompanies it remain always the one pedagogy of spiritual freedom and love.[42] The "zeal for justice," which a superior must never be without, must always go hand in hand with the "balm of mercy," which alone has the power to heal.[43] Only in this way can a monastic community, even one said to be of "strict observance," radiate the true spirit of the Gospel.

---

[39] See Aelred of Rievaulx, *Sermons for All Saints' Day*, sermon 10 (sermon 63 in the Reading-Cluny edition), cited by Raciti in "L'option préférentielle pour les faibles dans le modèle communautaire aelrédien."

[40] *Se non excipit a communi miseria, ne excipiatur a misericordia; Pharisaeus exsufflat misericordiam, dum dissimulat miseriam* (Bernard of Clairvaux, *GradHum* 5.17).

[41] Saint Bernard devoted his *De praecepto et dispensatione* to this topic.

[42] In this sense, the slogan that made its rounds through the Order during the 1970s and 1980s—"Passing from a spirituality of observances to a spirituality of charity"—needs to be completed. It is rather a matter of transforming the way of living the observances into a veritable pedagogy of spiritual freedom and love.

[43] See Bernard of Clairvaux, *CC* 12.14.

The Common Will

Just as the mercy of God and of the brothers is received and shared commonly by all, so does the knowledge of and the sharing in God's desire, both for the community as a whole and for each one of the brothers, become more refined: the monk learns to renounce his "self-will" and to discover the "common will." This insistence on the renunciation of all "property" goes further than simple obedience to the superior. It harks back to the primitive community in Acts 4:32 and encompasses all that would do harm to fraternal life or divide the community. In the first instance, of course, this pertains not only to private property of any sort but also to all forms of singularity, isolation from others, murmuring, and above all detraction, this last-mentioned vice being for Bernard the most evident sign of a flagrant lack of love.[44]

Obedience, a cenobitic virtue par excellence, equally takes on a "social" significance in the Cistercian climate. It is the design of God for the community that gives importance to communal discernment, a discernment for which total renunciation of self-will, by the brothers as well as by the abbot, is the indispensable condition. Community exchanges, offered in view of decisions to make, thus clothe themselves with an authentically spiritual value. They too form part of the school of love.

Pluriform Unity

This absence of all "property" in the negative sense of the word[45] and this quest for communion and for unity does not, however, exclude a healthy pluralism. Within the one Cistercian observance, the charisms are diverse. Bernard often repeated it: each monastery possesses its Marthas, its Marys, and even

---

[44] *Omnis qui detrahit, primum quidem seipsum prodit vacuum caritate* (Bernard of Clairvaux, *CC* 24.4). Bernard fears above all the communities where there reigns a *concordis discordia* and an *inimicissima amicitia* (*CC* 24.3-4).

[45] Baldwin of Ford, however, knows a *proprietas* that leads to *communio* (Baldwin of Ford, *The Common Life*, 10).

its Lazaruses,[46] likewise its Pauls and its Johns, cenobites, anchorites, gyrovagues, and even spiritual sarabaites, *officiales* and *claustrales*, both active members and contemplatives. The role of the abbot will be to encourage each particular vocation and to assure the unity of this diversity;[47] and the brothers' role will be to respect the diversity of the others without envy, at least so long as it does not affect the "better part" that all are invited to prefer. "Happy indeed is the community where Martha complains of Mary,"[48] says Saint Bernard who, under certain conditions, even encourages his brothers to carve out a modicum of solitude within the common life.[49] As has been rightly noted, "solitude and the common life become alternatives only when the community has degenerated into a totalitarian institution, demanding a uniform observance beyond what Saint Benedict would ever have envisaged."[50]

The communion among brothers is so total that each one of these particular vocations, and the graces it entails, becomes a common good. Within a community, "what belongs to one, belongs to all."[51] And this holds good in two ways, explains Baldwin of Ford: first, when the good that a brother possesses, he possesses for the other and, again, when he loves in the other the good that he does not possess himself: "Different graces are related to each other in communion when the gifts accorded separately to particular persons are possessed in common by the communion of love."[52] In a certain sense, for Bernard, belonging

---

[46] See Bernard of Clairvaux, *Sermons for the Assumption of the Virgin Mary* 3.4 (hereafter *Assum*); Bernard of Clairvaux, *Div* 90.3.

[47] *Div* 1.26.

[48] See Bernard of Clairvaux, *Assum* 3.2 and passim.

[49] See Bernard of Clairvaux, *CC* 40.4-5. On the other hand, a bad solitude is denounced in *Sermons for Candlemas* 2.2 (hereafter *Pur*).

[50] M. Casey, "*In communi vita fratrum*," 245.

[51] *Habent inter se talem unitatem et concordiam ut . . . quiquid est singulorum hoc est omnium, et quidquid est omnium, hoc est singulorum* (Aelred of Rievaulx, *Sermons for All Saints' Day* 26).

[52] See Baldwin of Ford, *The Common Life* 11.

to the community is a sufficient condition for salvation, even in the case of a monk who is "full of *acedia* and is the worst of all."[53]

Spiritual Friendship

If there had never been the celebrated treatise of Aelred, *On Spiritual Friendship*, it would have sufficed to look to the correspondence of Bernard and to many a confidence disclosed by his pen in order to gauge the extent to which the first Cistercians were given to a love of friendship. And this love of friendship can expand into love of God. Galland de Reigny confessed to Bernard how, in listening to him speak, his heart had filled with love for him, and he added: "I do well to say: of love for you, rather than of love for God. But by introducing itself into the mind, this love for you prepared a way to the love of God."[54]

Friendship presupposes a certain pedagogy that will not be the same for all ages. The greater or lesser affective maturity of the brother plays a determining role. All friendship is capable not only of favoring this maturity but also of arresting it or of leading it astray on paths where one does oneself harm. The birth of a friendship is, however, always an important event that merits respect and attention, whether it is a question of friendship between two persons living in the same cloister or with someone outside. At the beginning of monastic life, friendship demands an accompaniment based on a loyal openness of heart, for it is frequently called to become the way and the support of a greater love, for God and for the brothers. The way can be long. The *amor privatus* of the beginning must become the *amor communis*. Now it is obvious that, during a certain period, an intense affectivity, still insufficiently integrated, will play a role. Without overdramatizing possible excesses, the brother concerned ought to be unceasingly encouraged to love, not less, but rather more, and to *order* this love toward the preferential love for Jesus, in which his true vocation consists. Assisted in this

---

[53] Cited by Herbert of Clairvaux in his *De miraculis* 2.11, PL 185, 1323C.

[54] Galland de Reigny, *Second Letter to Bernard*, quoted in J. Leclercq, "The Parables of Galland de Reigny," *Analecta monastica* 1 (1948): 167–80.

way, the adventure of friendship can not only afford a real comfort but also become the test of the authenticity of love for God.

Cor unum et anima una: One Heart and One Soul

The breaking of the heart brings to birth in each of us new sight and a new spiritual sensibility. Mutual mercy and love, practiced with perseverance, causes the community ever more to resemble the celestial and even trinitarian communion of which it is the icon here below.[55] Even if the gifts of the individual monks are different and complementary, the exclusive devotion of all to the one and only God guarantees little by little the interior unity and unanimity of all. "Let the souls be one, let the hearts be united," exclaims Bernard, "in loving only one, in seeking only one, in adhering to only one, and in perceiving the same disposition in each one." Though activities may be different, "the interior unity and unanimity gather and bind together the differences themselves by the glue of charity and the bond of peace."[56]

It would be fitting to cite here in its entirety the detailed description, from the pen of William of Saint-Thierry, of this *specialis caritatis schola* that is the cenobitic life, where all instruction and all exchanges lead "not to reasoning but to the very truth and experience" of what they ponder: "Zeal and application to prayer are here so great and so continual that here every place becomes a place of prayer, a place where God reigns. . . . In the common exercises of piety, and even in a certain delight discernible in their faces, the brothers see in each other the presence of the divine kindness and they embrace one another with so much love that, like the Seraphim, each one sets the other afire with the love of God, and they can never get enough of what they bring to each other."[57]

---

[55] Without hesitation, Baldwin of Ford locates the source of cenobitic life in the life of heaven: "The common life is a certain splendor of the eternal light, an emanation of eternal life, an effluence from this perpetual spring out of which flow the living waters that well up to eternal life" (*The Common Life*, prologue); see from the same author, *De perfecto monacho*.

[56] See Bernard of Clairvaux, *Sermons for Septuagesima* 2.3.

[57] See William of Saint-Thierry, *NatDignAm* 25.

Excessus Contemplationis: The "Passage" to Contemplation

Beyond this fraternal communion, in which God is already mysteriously present, God alone can then, according to Bernard, take the initiative to call someone to the *excessus contemplationis*.[58] It is at this moment that that *Schola humilitatis*, the school of humility, bears all its fruit. Having already been guided by the Holy Spirit through the *cellars of fraternal charity*, and therefore languishing with love, the soul no longer waits to be admitted into the nuptial chamber of the King.[59] It is not a question here of a step by which the way of the contemplative life should necessarily come to full term. This is not within the reach of the monk, be he ever so zealous, even if it becomes ever more the exclusive desire of his heart. It belongs to God alone to "carry away" or to "ravish" the soul, says Bernard, with a term borrowed from Saint Paul's experience[60] (see 2 Cor 12:2-4), so as to introduce it for a brief moment into an experience that will be already a foretaste of eternal life.

But curiously, the soul never leaves, for all that, the humble way of the constraints of fraternal love which will never disappear entirely here below. Through them, the soul will never cease to return to the experience of its weakness. The school of love remains always a school of humility. The monk thus remains for a long time "a slow climber, a walker always fatigued, with a lazy foot, and who never stops inventing detours for himself."[61] But that does not matter. Of all the virtues that were Jesus', the Lord asked that we should learn only one from him: humility.[62] Bernard boldly writes that it is a happy and desirable weakness, therefore, that casts us unceasingly upon the grace and strength of God.[63] He confesses that it is in this way that he himself makes progress:

---

[58] See Bernard of Clairvaux, *GradHum* 6.19. *Excessus* remains difficult to translate and does not generally correspond to what recent mystical theology means by "ecstasy." The primary sense of *excedere* is "to pass outside or beyond."

[59] See *GradHum* 8.21.

[60] See Bernard of Clairvaux, *GradHum* 8.22.

[61] *GradHum* 9.24.

[62] See Matt 11:29, cited by Bernard of Clairvaux in *GradHum* 9.25.

[63] See Bernard of Clairvaux, *CC* 25.7.

Depending heavily on the foot of grace and slowly dragging my own, which is infirm, I will climb with assurance the ladder of humility until, clinging to the truth (God), I pass into the wide spaces of charity. It is thus that one progresses more prudently and, as it were, stealthily on a narrow way, and that one climbs more surely, and as if unawares, a ladder that is rough. It is in this astonishing fashion that one accedes to the truth (God), a bit slowly of course, but nevertheless all the more decisively—by limping.[64]

To make progress in love while dragging a bad foot, to climb while limping lazily: one could not find a more eloquent way of saying that the way to love passes always through humility. Our progress toward God by way of the community of brothers does not escape this fundamental law of the Gospel. Only the brother with a broken heart, aware of his poverty yet madly confident in mercy, can hope to arrive one day where God is waiting for him. "In any case," remarks Saint Bernard, "I recall having often repeated to you that our progress consists in this: to never think that we have arrived, but ever to bound ahead to what is before us, trying constantly to do better, and exposing continually all that is imperfect in us to the gaze of divine mercy."[65] In the context of Cistercian community, we can add: "and to the merciful eyes of our brothers."

---

[64] See Bernard of Clairvaux, *GradHum* 9.26.
[65] See Bernard of Clairvaux, *Sermons for Candlemas* 2.3.

4

Living in a Fraternal Community

God and Our Brother

Except in the case of hermits, religious life is always a life in community. This is not merely a factual given, imposed by the necessities of practical living; it is rather something inscribed in the nature of our vocation itself. Most of us discovered the call to religious life through contact with a concrete community that became familiar to us. In the comportment of these men living together as brothers in Jesus Christ, we recognized what we recognized in our hearts as a grace. To follow Jesus, we associated ourselves with a group of brothers. Since then, we have no longer been able to dissociate ourselves from these two realities: God and our brother. The bond with the one has reinforced the bond with the other: what we have done for the one, we have done for the other. Our commitment to follow Jesus, our final profession, was itself pronounced with our hands placed between the hands of a brother presiding over the community as its superior.

The New Code of Canon Law

In the new Code of Canon Law, promulgated on January 25, 1983, an entire canon is devoted to the "fraternal life" of religious. Significantly, it follows the canons concerning the three evangelical counsels of obedience, poverty, and chastity; this gives the impression that the common life is no less important than the three counsels, and that it too is directly related to the Gospel. By way of introduction, here is the text:

32

The life of brothers or sisters proper to each institute, by which all members are united together like a special family in Christ, is to be determined [in the constitutions of each institute] in such a way that it becomes a mutual support for all in fulfilling the vocation of each member. Moreover by their communion as brothers or sisters, rooted in and built on love, the members are to be an example of universal reconciliation in Christ.[1]

Perhaps these last words are the most important: by this fraternal communion, "the members are to be an example of universal reconciliation in Christ." In this text, fraternal communion is presented as an explicit mission on behalf of both the local and the universal Church.

A Bit of Vocabulary

Still by way of introduction, let us make some remarks about vocabulary. *Fraterna communio* ("fraternal communion") is a very ancient expression in monastic literature. When the common life, in the strict sense of the term, first appeared (according to current historical dating, this was in the fourth century, with Pachomius), the monastic community received a name derived from the New Testament: *hagia koinônia*, that is to say, a "holy communion," a "holy sharing." The term *koinônia* is borrowed from the Acts of the Apostles; it is the well-known description of the primitive Church: "They devoted themselves with one accord to the teaching of the apostles, to the common life (*koinônia*), to the breaking of the bread, and to the prayers" (2:42). The nature of this *koinônia* is specified in the verses that follow: common ownership of goods, communal frequentation of the Temple, unity of hearts and minds, and meals taken together with joy and sincerity of heart. And Saint Luke notes: "They enjoyed favor with all the people." In other words, the community radiated reconciliation in Jesus Christ.

---

[1] Canon 602, *Code of Canon Law*, Latin-English Edition (Washington, DC: Canon Law Society of America, 1983), 227.

Several centuries later, in the West, the monastic community for which Saint Benedict writes his Rule calls itself a *congregatio*. This might make us think of a "congregation" in the modern sense of the term, but this would be a mistake. In the Latin of Saint Benedict, *congregatio* is borrowed from the text of the Latin Vulgate. In Exodus and in the book of Numbers, *congregatio* is employed to designate the People of God on their march across the desert. It is a translation of the Hebrew term *qahal*, which became *ekklêsia* in the Greek text of the Septuagint, from which the word then passed into Latin in the sense of "Church." Saint Benedict therefore considers this monastic community as an event of the Church involving an ecclesial task.

The presentation that follows is divided into two parts:

- The Christian community is an ecclesial event, a divine event, a locus of grace.

- Some criteria for a Christian community.

The Christian Community Is an Event of the Church

THE LORD HIMSELF BUILDS HIS CHURCH

The first point to underline is the following: the Church of Jesus Christ (and every group within her) is gathered by the Lord himself. Saint Luke already noted this at the end of his description of the first Christian community: "And every day, the Lord added to the community those who would be saved" (Acts 2:47).

This remains true for every Christian community today. No one can start one up. No one can collaborate successfully to produce one by exerting his own strength. It must come from the divine initiative: the Lord himself builds his Church. Such indeed is our experience. It is not we who have chosen our brothers. In this time of vocational crisis, we are incapable of providing a remedy from our own resources. Nor have others coopted us. We went to knock at the door of a religious community because we thought we had a vocation, that is to say, we thought that the Lord was waiting for us on this monastic path.

The force that gathers and unites the Church, and every community within her, is found in God and has been concretely revealed to us in Jesus Christ. It begins to act from the start of Jesus' public ministry: he gathers disciples around him. A force of attraction emanates from him. It acts not only on those who seek a word or a cure from him but also on this little group that abandons family and nets and attaches itself to him to form the circle of his disciples. At its inception, it is no more than a provisional assemblage that knows its highs and lows, a constant coming and going. Some disciples join Jesus and, then again, some disciples leave him. At the moment of Jesus' passion and death, the group as such is put to the test and runs the risk of collapsing altogether, as Jesus himself had predicted: "The shepherd will be struck and the sheep will be scattered." We recall the scene: at Gethsemane, the apostles flee; Peter follows at a distance, hesitating, and then denies his Master; only John—miracle of miracles—will make it to Golgotha.

But this same group, dispersed and disunited, will once again be gathered and soldered into a Church by the death and the resurrection of Jesus. Caiaphas himself had prophesied it: "It is better that one man should die for the people." And Saint John remarks in this connection: "He prophesied that Jesus was to die for the nation, and not only for the nation, but to gather into one the dispersed children of God" (John 11:51). This gathering is the ultimate fruit of the paschal event: out of the world, Easter creates the Church. Everywhere that a community of the Church is formed, it can be nothing else but a fruit of the resurrection. It is but a first fruit, timid and fragile in our era, when the tension between dispersion and gathering, between *diaspora* and *ekklêsia*, constitutes an essential and permanent element; but this holds true equally each time that this tension is surmounted anew, provisionally, and, as it were, by anticipation, in the frail signs of the Church, of the *ekklêsia* of Jesus, which today consist of the ecclesial communities of the diocese, the parish, the family, and the religious community.

The Church: Plenitude and Diaspora

In order to realize community, the Church absolutely does not need to be imposing, numerically important, astonishing. Indeed, to the contrary, everything was already given at the foot of the Cross. The *ekklêsia* was then reduced to Mary, John, the converted sinful woman, the holy women, and also that pagan, the Roman centurion who confessed the divinity of Jesus, and finally the good thief, who preceded all the others into the kingdom of God. It is noteworthy that neither Peter nor the other apostles are there. Peter is not, however, absent; his mode of presence is peculiar. At this hour, he is given over to weeping, entirely turned around by the gaze of Jesus. As at Golgotha, the Church is also present in the upper room of the Cenacle on Pentecost: Mary, John, Peter, the other apostles, and the rest of the disciples. All is already given in this little seed.

Today, we have nothing in addition to this. It is for us, today, neither easier nor more difficult to form a Christian community. Our Church knows the same tensions as formerly: these are, still today, among the characteristics of the Church. The latter has already received the plenitude, the *plerôma*; she lives in perpetual tension between dispersion and fullness. This tension is necessary and will never cease until the end of time. Today, the Church is nothing, and yet, at the same time, she saves the world; she is worthless in the eyes of the world and nevertheless constitutes the salvation of the whole human race.

It has sometimes been a temptation for the Church (and perhaps equally for us today) to draw up statistics and, above all, to attach a certain importance to these statistics. The fervor of the Church is not to be measured by the number of baptisms, communions, and so forth, that one tallies up in the hope that these numbers will be as high as possible. In fact, that is a completely erroneous way to say anything worthwhile about the Church of Jesus. In the Old Testament, King David was severely punished for an attempt of this kind. He wanted to know exactly the might of the People of God and he decreed a census to that end. In the eyes of God, such a gesture was deprived of any significance. The

Church will always be small in some sense—a bit of leaven in the dough, a mustard seed—and yet powerful enough to effectively save the whole world. The Church is *diaspora*, dispersion, minority, and she is *plerôma*: she is the fullness of the power of Jesus.

It will only be at the end of time, when Christ will return and God will be all in all, that there will be no more *diaspora*. At that time, Jesus tells us, the angels will be sent to gather the elect from the four corners of the world at the sound of the trumpets (Matt 24:31). Then the *plerôma* of the Church, her plenitude, will coincide with the universe, with the entire world. It is only then that there will no longer be any world outside of the Church. Before the end of time, any attempt to somehow approximate this result, or to give the appearance of so doing, is doomed to failure. In fact, the true situation of the Church in the world is the opposite of this dream, and this is in conformity with the salvific design of Jesus himself. Of course, the Church has been sent into the world by Jesus to proclaim the good news, but the result of this proclamation will not be her triumphing over the world, or annexing it to herself, or taking its place. The Church, before the parousia, will not occupy every territory in the world. She lives in *diaspora*, in the midst of the world, like a hidden but revelatory sign of that which, one day, will come to be. There are little groups within the Church that emerge and become visible more or less everywhere and that are signs of the salvation that they enact by their very nature: places of charity, of peace, of prayer, of divine life, of communion.

The Community: Sign of Gratuity and Mercy

From the foregoing there follows an important consequence for the theological situation (if I may so express myself) of a Christian community. What is our situation as a community? Man left to himself is not capable of living in community. His normal condition is life in *diaspora*, in dispersion in the midst of the world, separated from others and, more profoundly, from himself. This being so, a Christian community, wherever it comes to birth, can only be a gift, a sign of the mercy of God, an anticipation, a prefigurement and foretaste of the kingdom that is to come, of that which, only later, will be a reality for the whole Church. The Christian community is always something prospective: a window opening out to heaven.

We can somewhat compare it to the situation of the apostle John, exiled on the island of Patmos. There he is, isolated, alone on his rock, fully in *diaspora*. By faith, however, he is linked to the whole Church. Still, he does not become truly aware of this until a certain Sunday. On that day John has a vision. A door in heaven opens for him, and there he contemplates already the deepest reality of the Church to which he is vitally connected here at Patmos: all the elect gathered around the throne of God and of the Lamb. An ecclesial community is always comparable to such a Sunday, for it is a moment when a window opens in heaven, witnessing to the world about what will one day come to pass.

A community is therefore an "apocalypse," that is to say, a revelation. It tells the Church and the world of the bonds that unite all in Christ and in God. A community is also "eschatological": it offers even now a glimpse of what will be fully realized at the eschaton, at the end of time. Hence it is evident that the Christian community is always a locus of grace. It is a prodigy that God manifests in this world today. The community is never a human work. We do not have such a right. In a certain sense, we do not belong to this community any more than it belongs to us. It is for us to receive it as a gift of God, in the face of which we must always maintain a welcoming stance and to which we must always open ourselves ever more.

But we also experience each day the risk of being excluded from the community. Not that God may reject us or that others may spurn us: the others wait for us and God does the same; but we risk detaching ourselves little by little from the community. Perhaps unconsciously, we try to guide the community in our own way. Maybe we impose ourselves on it. Perhaps it has become with time a part of ourselves: our work, our source of pride, our affair. If we were to find ourselves in such a state, this would increase for us the risk of being thrown back into our own isolation, which would have happened long ago for each one of us but for the unshakable mercy and fidelity of God. For it is upon his love and faithfulness that every Christian community is founded.

In the ritual for entrance into a monastic community, the postulant enters the chapter room and prostrates before abbot and community. The superior asks him this question: "What do you seek?" The response is: "The mercy of God and of the Order." This expresses well the profound meaning of what is happening. In every Christian community, we enter by the little door and must therefore make ourselves very little. In the depths of our heart we must remain thus, for all our days: prostrate before our brothers, in the same hope and with the same prayer on our lips, imploring the mercy of God and of our brothers.

Some Criteria for the Christian Community

The Christian community is thus a locus of grace, a divine work, a miracle for whose realization we must unceasingly pray. The question therefore arises: But where can the Christian community be found? How can I recognize it? More precisely: Does the Christian community coincide with what we today call "the community phenomenon" and with any form of this phenomenon? The experience of daily life, familiar to us in religious life, is such that we know very well that such a phenomenon is not always a miraculous affair. In such a group, I find myself more or less at ease, more or less in my element, I feel more or less accepted. Every group has its lights and its shadows. There are equally days and times during which I feel as if submerged in these shadowy aspects. The result of this is that I surprise myself—I speak for myself here—criticizing the common life. I am not always gentle in my assessment of the brothers, nor of the superior. And then we ask: Is this really legitimate? What does it mean? If the Christian community exists on the plane of the miraculous, of the saving action of God, does that mean that every criticism thereof comes from the Evil One and would in some way be an attack on the goodness and the mercy of God? Such is certainly not my intention when I criticize what happens in community. I feel that my critique can even be positive and that I sometimes have the right to speak my mind. This shows us already that the community phenomenon and the ecclesial community are not, if the truth be told, reducible one to the other.

Besides, it is obvious—above all today—that every group has not only a negative side that is the source of difficulties but also a banal side that is completely ordinary and profoundly human. In our days, thanks be to God, we are much better informed in this area by the sociology and psychology of groups. We possess much more extensive information on the structure of the group, on the norms and customs to which every human group conforms, as it were, by natural necessity. The forces and desires that live in each person are likewise reflected in the group and are somehow tied together there. They can evolve in a positive way so long as they are judiciously directed by the common life and by dialogue. But they can also develop negatively and overwhelm the life of the group, demolish it, and render it almost impossible. "Hell is other people," Sartre has said famously.

Thanks to this increase of knowledge, it is possible for us to improve the life of the group and to try to direct it onto better paths. Such a group can be sick, but it can also be healed. In the case of a group that is fundamentally healthy and functioning in a way that is completely correct, this can become an important factor in the healing of an individual's life. Likewise, groups have become such bearers of life that we speak of "group therapy." This is without question an important acquisition of our modern culture.

But here another question arises. What is the relation between the good functioning of a group *qua* group and a Christian community that is an event of the Church? And, if they should have something in common, do they overlap entirely? In other words: Is a group Christian and conformed to the gospel in the measure that it functions well as a group? And conversely: If a group is explicitly inspired by the gospel, does it necessarily follow that it will function well as a group? In actual fact, we are dealing here with a classic question that we recognize from other contexts. What is the relationship between nature and grace? The response to this type of question is never simple, never unilateral: it is never an alternative between two options. It is always a delicate task to express the matter in the abstract, on the level of principles. Properly speaking, what is required is *diakrisis*, a discernment of spirits, a discernment by the Holy Spirit, the interior sensitivity that the Spirit gives us for perceiving the life of God in us and in others.

Now, this life of God is made known by certain manifest signs. The Word of God in the Bible and the experience of twenty centuries of ecclesial life have borne witness to the value of these signs. Let us therefore say a few words on the criteria of a Christian community. We will first enumerate them:

- The Christian community is built upon human weakness.
- The Christian community is a place of forgiveness.
- The Christian community is a place of healing.

THE CHRISTIAN COMMUNITY IS BUILT ON HUMAN WEAKNESS

Let us listen to Saint Paul in his First Letter to the Corinthians:

> Again, brothers, consider your call. Not many among you were wise according to the flesh. Not many of you were powerful, nor were many of you well-born. But God has chosen what the world considers foolish in order to confound the wise. He has chosen those who are weak in this world in order to confound the strong. God has chosen those who are lowly and despised, those who count for nothing, to reduce to nothing those who are something so that no flesh might boast before God. For it is because of him that you are in Christ Jesus who, according to God's will, has become for us wisdom and justice, sanctification and redemption. (1 Cor 1:26-30)

God chose us on account of our weakness and, in a completely concrete manner, at our weakest point, so to speak, at our deepest vulnerability, in order to heal it by his power and to make of it the cornerstone, the foundation, of his Church. That has always been his way of acting in salvation history. This was already the case for the People of God in the desert. Let us think of Deuteronomy:

Why is Israel the chosen people? Not because it is powerful, great, or faithful, but because it is the smallest, the least of all peoples (Deut 7:7).

This littleness and this vulnerability can manifest themselves in every domain: material means, social status, number, intellectual capacity. . . . A Christian community is always close to those who are disabled in any sense. That is true of our most basic weakness, of our condition as sinners, of our continual poverty vis-à-vis the inexhaustible grace and mercy of God. But this weakness poses no obstacle at all. It is precisely because of it that God has chosen us, with this wound and this weakness, for the realization of his work. God needs this weakness so that his power at work in the Church may manifest itself in all its plenitude.

The fundamental weakness on account of which God has chosen us also defines our relationship with our brothers. They did not accept us because of our human and spiritual qualities. There was no entrance examination. No! In a community that lives the Gospel, it has been granted us to enter with our weaknesses, indeed almost because of them. We have been accepted just as we are, as a gift from God. In Christ Jesus our weakness is a gift to the community. For every weakness reveals something of the strength and the love of God.

We, in turn, have not selected others according to whatever demanding norms we may espouse. We, too, have divined their weakness, such as it presents itself day by day, veiled, healed, and restored by the power of God. While acting in this way, we have recognized their poverty and weakness as a sign of the love of God and we have been able to welcome them with gratitude as a gift of God.

One could always object: Is this really true? Do things really transpire thus? For example, when we vote on the definitive admission of a novice, do things unfold according to these criteria? We accept someone for his qualities and we refuse others because we judge that certain faults are incompatible with religious life. I may concede this up to a certain point, but I must nonetheless underline that such cannot be the final and decisive criterion for determining whether or not to accept a brother into a community that lives the Gospel. Everyone has good qualities and defects. The determining question is, rather: How does this man behave in the face of these gifts and faults? If a candidate is presented who is richly talented but also unconsciously given to imposing his riches on the group, we can remove him with a tranquil conscience. On the other hand, a candidate who is burdened with heavy personal baggage but who is aware of his frailties and is, in a certain sense, reconciled to them, and who knows by experience that he can unceasingly confess God's mercy toward him in his weakness: such a one we accept with thanksgiving, precisely because this experience of the mercy of God will translate in him sooner or later into a merciful tenderness toward everyone.

Again, and for the same reason, it is important to be able to look squarely at the weaknesses of the group and to have opportunities for doing so, for these are precisely the important points for its spiritual growth. I have the impression that we often maintain the reverse policy. All that could provoke disturbance or scandal is carefully hidden and veiled. The community, such as it is, is placed very high up, emphatically idealized, and this ideal is the unconscious expectation of all its members. Whoever does not manage to live up to this expectation is held at a distance and sometimes loses the love and trust of the superiors or the brothers. This is really unfortunate, for in this way we favor a process that runs entirely contrary to the dynamism of the Holy Spirit and of a Christian community living out the Gospel. The community thus risks becoming a kind of sect, gathering perfectly trained, elite recruits—"the pure and the tough"—who will keep themselves at a distance from the common run of mortals and ordinary Christians.

To be mistaken about the deep reality of the community is a very common fault among beginners who enter the community with a very exalted ideal. They suppose themselves to have discovered a dream community, but this dream exists only in their imagination, in the unconscious image of the perfection of their own "me." Yet the reality is completely different. And what is still more surprising is that God himself permits the reality to be completely different and that he does not wish that it should ever correspond to the dreamed-up image of an ideal community. For this reason, each one of us must be disappointed by our own community. It is an inevitable and unsparing disappointment but salutary as well. It is a very instructive frustration, even though it may take some time to integrate. The pain it causes is unbearable: one becomes bitter, caustic toward others, severe toward the group, judging, and condemning. Criticism becomes razor sharp. One has it in for everybody, especially for the Church, since the human reality that they offer us does not correspond to the ideal that we anticipated. This means that they are not the screen behind which we could shelter our weakness. Through the faults of the other members as well as those of the whole group, we perceive that we are implicated in the same deficiencies. We are not better than the others. And they do not succeed at making us better. But that is not the real issue here. Indeed, we should identify ourselves with the others in our common frailty in order to reach, from this point of departure, the salvation given by Jesus. *De profundis*—"Out of the depths." For this is the Good News, this is the Church, and nothing else. Jesus came for these sinners, these sinners that in fact we are, and not for the righteous that we thought we were, that we hoped to become or appear to be, secure at the heart of the Christian community. There is no Good News without the proclamation of the forgiveness of sin.

I speak of a salutary disillusionment, an enriching frustration. God has willed it so. For grace must become grace and not that something we could claim as our due, to which we would have a right if we fulfilled certain conditions. We cannot fulfill even the least condition. Herein lies the foundation of the community that lives together because of Jesus Christ and the salvation that is in him.

It is this that we must grasp first of all, and this knowledge is gained neither through a demonstration nor through study; it comes only through sheer grace. Once we receive the gift of understanding, everything is given us at a single stroke, even here and now, whatever may be the group in which we are now living. Dietrich Bonhoeffer said: "From the moment we cease to dream about community, community is at once granted us"; and this is the Church of Jesus, built upon our weakness.

This is why it is so important that we not downplay our weakness before our brothers. They can learn something from our shortcomings. We ought to be able to share, not everything, but at least some of our difficulties. We must not steal away. We must not be afraid to lose face. It can be a formidable support for our brothers to know that we too are weak, that we are not heroes at all. This was perhaps the meaning behind the practice that, in our tradition, we knew formerly under the name of "chapter of faults" and that we seek today to replace with forms better adapted to modernity (without much success, it must be confessed). The deep truth of a group resides in the fact that the brothers transmit to each other something on the level of fault-and-pardon: this is the sole and unique means that God employs to make of this group his own society. It is the evangelical atmosphere of the group. In such an encounter, we breathe God's air, if I may put it thus, and the life of God.

I think that the superior can himself, too, allow some of his fragility to show. He too is a forgiven sinner. And if, by chance, he was not such or thought he was not, he would have no motive for remaining superior much longer. He could not satisfy the minimal condition of being able to announce to the others what he owes to the mercy of God. Paul wrote to his disciple Timothy: "Christ came into the world to save sinners, of which I am the foremost" (1 Tim 1:15). Paul thus confesses that he is, among the apostles, as one untimely born, the one who is not worthy of being called "apostle." But what he is, he is by grace. Paul has authority in the Church. And it is because he was able to have, in his own person, the experience of grace, that he is all the more able to share it with others.

The same holds true for Peter. He was the first to experience the forgiveness of Jesus. He denied him, yet he is the first of the apostles to whom Jesus appears on the very day of his resurrection. This constitutes, as you know, the most ancient *kerygma*. When the two disciples of Emmaus return to Jerusalem, they are told: "The Lord has truly been raised and has appeared to

Simon!" The first appearance of the risen Christ to an apostle is made to Simon who had denied him. And before Peter, who was to be vested with authority, there was Mary Magdalene, the forgiven sinner who, on Easter morning, saw the Risen One in the garden and was charged with announcing it to Peter and to the apostles who, however, did not believe her.

The superior is not capable of being truly a superior unless, at a given moment, he has found himself at the weak point, the fragile place of the community. For, in the Christian community, it is always the weakest members who are at the heart and the center. And that gives the Christian community a very particular aspect, its proper atmosphere that departs markedly from the dynamic of every other group that is not resolutely evangelical. For, in every human group, there exists a field of tensions composed of desires and ambitions that cross each other, often conflict with each other, but must seek to enter into harmony.

In the best of circumstances these tensions resolve themselves in the person of the leader who creates unity and harmony. Every group is thus constituted hierarchically: it looks to the highest point, toward the summit, and clings to the leader who is the emanation and the symbol of the group.

The same holds true, up to a point, for communities that live according to the Gospel. And yet . . . in a community following the Gospel, another dynamic enters into play, for the pyramid is here inverted. The center of gravity, the focal point, is the lowest point, the little one, the weak one. One does not give one's exclusive attention to the leader, but everyone, including the leader, is solicitous for the weakest member and, together with the others, carries the weakest member. The superior is the one best positioned to look after the weak ones. The image of the abbot in the Rule of Saint Benedict is that of the good shepherd who leaves the other sheep and goes in search of the lost sheep in order to carry it home on his shoulders and restore it to the sheepfold. The superior is someone who can give evidence of the greatest love, the greatest tenderness. He is someone who can humble himself, who can make himself little, who, after the example of Jesus, can kneel before others and wash their feet.

The two other points of which we now treat are but a consequence of what we have said above.

A PLACE OF FORGIVENESS AND RECONCILIATION

Let us now listen to a short passage from Saint Paul's Letter to the Colossians:

> You, therefore, who are God's elect, holy and beloved, must clothe yourselves with tender compassion, with benevolence, humility, gentleness, and patience; bear with one another and forgive one another if anyone of you has a grievance against another. . . . Finally, above everything else, put on charity, which is the bond of perfection. And may the peace of Christ reign in your hearts, for to this peace you have been called and gathered as one body. Dedicate yourselves to thanksgiving! (3:12-15)

Only weakness can serve as the foundation for the group because it is in this weakness that the strength of God can manifest itself. And the power of God manifests itself best in forgiveness. Here we may recall the ancient Latin collect: *Deus qui omnipotentiam tuam parcendo maxime et miserando manifestas.* . . . God manifests his "omnipotence above all in showing mercy and forgiveness." Forgiveness is the glue of community: it binds us together because it is the very life of God flowing in the veins of the Church. Forgiveness is not weakness, nor capitulation before sin, nor camouflaged complicity with sin. Forgiveness is the essential dynamic of salvation. "Where sin abounded, grace has abounded all the more." Forgiveness is the triumph of love, stronger than all sin. In this sense, forgiveness is edifying, literally "upbuilding," constructive.

Only God can forgive sin, but his forgiveness is revealed to us through others. Not only in the sacrament of penance—that is one particular situation—but also from morning to evening, through the whole life of our community. It comes to us through others. And because we experience it through others, we can likewise communicate it, transmit it, to others. The life and growth of a community are entirely tied to this event of salvation brought by the Gospel. In the light of this experience, the concrete tasks that we must eventually assume as a community are only secondary. For *forgiveness is the fundamental experience of the Christian community*.

To learn to place oneself within the community in this way, forgiven by God and forgiving others in turn, is a gift that is granted us only over the long haul. There are so many roots of ambition, aggression, hatred, and destruction that we carry in our hearts and that can only be uprooted over a long period of time, as the fruit of faithful and patient love. Jesus himself discloses to us the treasures of love that have accumulated in his Church and in the hearts of our brothers, as well as in our own hearts. This is the secret of the Church, the secret of God's heart. Our brothers love us as we truly are and not as we should be, nor as they wish us to be, nor as we wish us to be. But they love us in our weakness, in our sin. Paul says it explicitly: the proof that God truly loves us is that, on our behalf, he delivered his Son up to death, while we were still sinners (Rom 5:8). Experiencing love in this manner, we can transmit love and forgiveness to others in turn. Everyone has the right to be who he is and such as he is. The group does not impose on him from outside, as a condition, a model of life. All that is best and most profound within him will rise spontaneously to the surface provided that it is cultivated, encouraged, and developed by love.

This *nimia caritas* of God, this profusion—this superabundance of love that founds the Church upon forgiveness—equally founds every Christian community. It must be able to freely circulate therein. It is the very life of God, and outside of this life there is not Church, or community, or creative love.

It is in this way that sinners must have a privileged place in the community. I would even say: a place reserved. They are expected there. A Christian community that does not include defective persons is simply unthinkable. Not only is it impossible, it is not even desirable. In a place where sin has become absolutely unthinkable, or is completely covered up, grace has nothing more to do. We would then be living in another world, a world without redemption, a world without salvation; we would be living, in fact, in an illusion, the illusion of the Pharisees.

THE CHRISTIAN COMMUNITY IS ALSO A COMMUNITY OF HEALING

We find here once again the same concept that we noted a moment ago, one that comes to us from the modern psychology of groups. By its very nature and necessarily, a Christian community involves group therapy. From the very fact that a Christian community is fundamentally built upon forgiveness, it is also essentially a form of group therapy. Perhaps the group will inflict wounds and reveal the wounds we have hidden within ourselves. Also, it often happens that shortly after we have become members of a group someone points out to us our deficiencies! But in addition, it is the role of the group to cauterize these wounds and to heal them. This comes about through forgiveness. Forgiveness heals because forgiveness always presupposes a superabundance of love, a *nimia caritas*, an "excessive love," a love driven to distraction. For our sin is never anything but a frustrated love, a disappointed love, an embittered love, a love that has turned itself into hate. That is why the most radical healing is administered in the encounter with a love that is total, pure, disinterested, and that is God—God such as he is in the Church of Jesus: a love that heals, that looks after, that saves, that enables flourishing, that edifies.

We are sometimes given to think that, when we easily dispense forgiveness, we encourage sin in one way or another. And we are hence led to justify a certain severity, a rigor in governance. One cannot close one's eyes too readily, we think, else lenience will be abused. I believe that all that is true, but only in the measure that forgiveness does not issue from an authentic love but simply from condescension or from weakness, which likewise happens. But here I am speaking only of authentic love, in the image of God's love, and this love is *strong in forgiveness*. Such forgiveness, which is a grace and a miracle of God, is also constructive. We can only transmit it if it is granted to us that we, ourselves, abide in God's forgiveness. Only then will we be able to communicate love, a love that is so full, so surpassing even for the sinner, that I daresay it makes repulsive any thought of returning to sin. Here one discovers the irresistible force of the love of God expressed in forgiveness.

Thus, love sets us free. Love unseals in us the source of our true freedom. We do not act freely except in the measure that we act in love, placing ourselves in the love of someone who loves us and then sharing, in turn, the love we have received. This is the experience in a Christian community. Just as we can heal, thanks to others, so too can we, thanks to others, become free. The one who refrains from condemning others will thus evoke the best of what is in them, delivering them from shame and guilt feelings, enabling their deepest identity to bloom freely.

Saint-Exupéry has written somewhere: "A friend is, first of all, someone who does not judge." This does not imply endorsing all that is done, but rather that one truly refuses to judge. It is not our place to judge. Notwithstanding his faults, we welcome the brother as he is, in love. He will find a place here even with his sins because he is better than his sins. And our love will give pride of place to "the better part" within him.

Authentic Human Freedom Springs Forth from within the Community's Love

In this authentic human liberty which emerges from love, there also emerge the best qualities of the person. I mean that here the unique gift of each one of our brothers is revealed, and this seems to me extremely important. For each one of us who lives in a group patterned on the Gospel has received from God an extraordinary charism to build up the Church, to become a co-founder of the community. Each one of us has a spark of genius; in every other way we may be very ordinary, but in this one thing we are endowed with genius. And what is remarkable in us is a gift of God for the service of others.

This spark of genius is not linked to our formation, or to our studies, or to our diplomas. Sometimes it exists on a level other than that of our daily tasks. Only the true love of the community is capable of discovering our particular aptitude. It is of the utmost importance for each one of us that we be recognized by others for this particular gift that, perhaps, we ourselves do not suppose we possess and of which we are often doubtful. In conclusion, I will reread the text of Saint Paul from Colossians 3 and then we will conclude with a prayer:

> Bear with one another and forgive one another, if any one of you has a grievance against another. The Lord has forgiven you, now you must do the same. Finally, above all else, put on charity, which is the bond of perfection. And may the peace of Christ reign in your hearts: for it was to this peace that all of you were called into one body. Dedicate yourselves to thanksgiving!

Lord Jesus, we thank you for the grace that you never cease to give to your Church. You have called us together. You build your Church within our community. We thank you for weakness, this profound weakness that you alone know, that you alone can reveal to us. Our weakness is discovered in your strength. For this reason, we give you thanks.

5

Obedience in the Monastic Tradition

To try to reconstruct the history of spiritual obedience by moving back over the course of the ages, from the Rule of Saint Benedict to the New Testament, would be an exhilarating enterprise. A minute examination of the documents of primitive monasticism or of premonastic ascetical literature would hold surprises for us. But such cannot be the task undertaken in these few pages.

It would have been simpler to analyze obedience as it presents itself in the Rule of Saint Benedict, this document of the sixth century that, in the West, progressively became the fundamental and unique charter of hidden monastic life. But it is possible to do more. While using this Rule as our principal point of departure, we will read it continually in the light of the monastic tradition in which it is rooted. It will suffice to elicit from the tradition certain basic constants to describe diverse spiritual situations in which, in one way or another, obedience comes to the fore.

In order to do this, we must maintain a certain reserve with regard to the notion of "religious obedience" commonly accepted until just before Vatican II. This is not done with the intention of contesting such a conception but in order better to isolate from an excessive systematization the permanent values that are the immediate heritage of the great tradition.

Sociological Obedience and Charismatic Obedience

One of the characteristics of religious obedience consists in a certain identification of sociological obedience with charismatic obedience proper. Here we may sum up, in a few simple words, the doctrine of obedience that can be styled "classic." The person making the vow of obedience does it always into the hands of a superior, to whose person he is concretely vowed. Through this superior, however, the obedience is addressed to God, of whom the leader of the community is the recognized representative. At the same time, the superior guarantees the authenticity of the will of God that is manifested in the decisions he makes. In obeying his legitimate superior, the religious cannot err. The superior thus becomes in some sense the depository of the will of God, on condition that his orders contradict neither good morals nor the commandments of the Church nor the approved constitutions of the order.

Obedience conceived in this way is demanding. It presupposes a great love. It was, however, more commonly linked to the virtue of religion inasmuch as its purpose was to pay homage to God by the offering of what is most precious in man: his freedom.[1]

The tendency to identify spiritual obedience with sociological obedience would seem to have appeared very early in the history of monastic life, in practice from the time that cenobitic life first began to take shape. But the absorption of one sort of obedience by the other is not yet a *fait accompli* in the Rule of Benedict, which extends obedience to other persons besides the abbot.[2] By contrast, in the thirteenth century, in someone like Saint Thomas for example, the obedience of the hermit living in solitude creates difficulties precisely for the fact that he has no superior available.[3] The centuries that followed only accentuated all the more this reduction in which the most vital aspects of spiritual obedience have been progressively concealed.

Is the charismatic nature of obedience safeguarded in such a reduction? Is one not bound to obey the leader of a group simply by dint of one's participation in that group? In effect, each group

---

[1] *Summa Theologiae*, II^a II^{ae}, q. 88, a. 5.
[2] See RB 71.1: "That the Brothers Should Show Mutual Obedience."
[3] *Summa Theologiae*, II^a II^{ae}, q. 188, a. 8, ad 3. See J. Winandy, "Le sens original des conseils évangéliques," *Collectanea Cisterciensia* 22 (1960): 105–9.

has, along with its own common good, an internal discipline to which ordinary common sense and a natural exigency invite and even constrain the members to submit.

On the other hand, an acute perception of secularization could induce us to pose several questions concerning the supernatural motivation that a superior imagines he must introduce so that his orders may be respected. Does not sociological obedience, of whatever kind, possess its own coherence and dynamic that ought not to be interfered with by other norms, as in the case of a supernatural motivation artificially brought in from outside?

Such questions ought not to surprise us. They bring to light the extent to which it is important to distinguish between a purely social obedience and the charism properly called "spiritual obedience." It will perhaps be useful here to reconstruct the true form of the charism of obedience, after having dissociated it from that social obedience which, in fact, it contains in the majority of cases.

How to define the charism of obedience? A glance at some closely related charisms, such as those of celibacy and poverty, is instructive. A charism is understood as a spiritual good belonging to the kingdom. It therefore represents a paschal situation that prolongs in the Church a particular trait of the physiognomy of Christ. This good pertains to all Christians, in the present, and in a certain manner they recognize in it a profound orientation that is within them by the gift of the Holy Spirit. But only certain Christians—let us call them charismatics—are called to embrace the plenitude of this charism as of now. Incarnating with a certain urgency, and even with a certain folly, a particular good of the kingdom, they become as it were the sign of the proximity of this good and of its presence hidden in the heart of the Church while it is still in this world.

In the sense that we have just explained, celibacy can be seen clearly as a charism, in contrast to a purely social obedience. Social obedience is a necessity of the present time and does not belong exclusively to the kingdom that is to come. It is not free and cannot therefore constitute the object of a preferential choice. In this regard, Christ did not find himself in a unique situation compared to that of others. He too owed obedience to the authorities of his time. Finally, social obedience does not distinguish Christians from one another. In itself it is only the sign of a spiritual reality in which the whole of the Christian people participate in varying degrees.

Yet the spiritual obedience that appears in the New Testament and in the ancient documents possesses a notably different visage, one with multiple and complementary traits from which the monastic tradition has progressively been able to draw profit, linking them always in an explicit fashion to the example left among us by the Lord Jesus.

In trying now to specify these traits, we will focus above all on the study of three types of *spiritual situations* to which correspond three different types or graces of obedience: obedience as self-abasement, obedience as docility (or "discernment"), and prophetic (or apostolic) obedience. After having studied them separately, we will then have to see how this triple grace is lived concretely within the form of cenobitic obedience such as Saint Benedict presents it and as monks still try to live it today.

Obedience as Self-Abasement

To speak of self-abasement or humility is to touch on the most striking originality of the gospel message. Now, even in the most ancient texts, this self-abasement is set in relation to a certain kind of obedience. Obviously, the first Christians did not discover this relation by reasoning on some notion of humility. Only the concrete example of Christ permitted them to achieve an approximation that had never entered the mind of any pagan philosopher. We have a privileged testimony of this, probably the most ancient, in the famous christological hymn of the letter to the Philippians. To recommend humility, Saint Paul here recalls the example of Jesus who "abased himself, becoming obedient unto death, death on a cross" (Phil 2:8). In chapter 5 of the letter to the Romans, he opposes the obedience of Christ to the disobedience of Adam. After the refusal of Adam, the way to God must be opened up again. As head of a new humanity, Jesus presents an act of obedience that opens once again the road on which all human beings will henceforth be able to make their way. In this sense, Christ's self-abasement through his obedience is essential to Christian grace. Every Christian is invited to embrace it and to reach his fulfillment by means of it.

But it will not happen in the same way for all. There are particular situations that are valuable as signs and there are charisms that correspond to them. Saint Paul knows at least one particular social situation in which certain Christians find themselves called to witness to the grace of obedience, and that is slavery. The counsels that he gives to Christian slaves are strange to our modern sensibilities. For him, however, they naturally recommend themselves. Was not Christ, in his self-abasement, essentially a servant?

A situation of slavery freely entered into because of Christ is not without resemblance to the state of subjection for which the monk opts in religious obedience. In the two cases, a state of inferiority is freely embraced the better to confess Christ and the paschal realities that already belong to us. If we are all slaves by reason of Christ's self-abasement, it is all the more fitting to remain in a state of social subjection. If we are all united in Christ, what motive is there for leaving a state of inferiority? Above all, it puts us in a position the better to confess the grace that was his and to incarnate concretely the self-abasement that he embraced for our salvation (cf. Eph 6:5-9; Col 3:22–4:1).

In the most ancient documents of premonastic asceticism, obedience is mentioned little, in contrast to humility, which already had an honored place alongside virginity, prayer, fasting, and vigils. Several centuries later, as monastic life evolved little by little, obedience came to be seen as linked to the self-abasement of Christ; it expresses the desire to continue his humility and to share in his passion.[4]

---

[4] A very ancient witness—perhaps the most ancient—of this conjunction between obedience and humility is *The Book of Steps*, a Syriac document from Asia Minor that probably dates from the beginning of the fourth century. The addressees of this document are not yet monks in the strict sense of the word but rather itinerant ascetics who walk along the roads in a state of absolute poverty. One of their favorite virtues is humility, which expresses itself most

This link between the obedience and the humility of Christ was to become a commonplace of the tradition. It translated into the desire to live a hidden life of self-abasement expressed in the search for a condition of subjection to others. This attraction is not exclusively monastic. It belongs to the grace of baptism. But the part of the monk is to cultivate it with a particular insistence. Guided by his spiritual instinct, the monk systematically gives preference to a state of self-abasement of whatever kind. To be subject to a superior is one possible type of self-abasement, but there are many others. One thinks automatically of the very monastic affirmation of Charles de Foucauld: "Jesus took the last place so radically that no one can any longer take it from him."

In the Rule of Benedict, obedience holds as great a place as humility. When Benedict sets up his famous ladder of humility,[5] he reserves the first four degrees to a quadruple progress in obedience: to obey God in view of the divine reward or punishments; to take pleasure in renouncing self-will in order to do God's will, after the example of Christ. Only at the third degree does the superior finally appear and, with him, an obedience of the social type: "The third degree is to submit to a superior, with all obedience, out of love for God," whereas the fourth degree of humility, celebrated among us, describes the most critical moment and the summit of such obedience: "When one finds oneself imposed upon by hard and contrary things, indeed by injustices of every sort . . . , one does not give way to discouragement or draw back." The proof of strength in a cenobite—the heart of his ascesis—is almost always situated in obedience. It is the Benedictine "night" par excellence. After a fifth degree devoted to the disclosure of one's conscience, the following degrees present the traits of humility and self-effacement that specify the

---

frequently in a delicate charity toward all and particularly toward their persecutors. In at least one passage (25.7), the author counsels the ascetics to submit to others in order thus to express the humility of Christ. (The Syriac text, accompanied by a Latin translation, was published in 1926 by O. Kmosko in *Patrologia Syriaca*, v. 1 [Paris: Firmin-Didot et Socii, 1926]. This edition was later replaced by the *Patrologia Orientalis*.)

[5] See RB 7.

form of obedience according to Saint Benedict. The monk will be content with all disagreeable conditions and even with every extreme to which he may find his life reduced. In the tasks he performs under obedience, he will consider himself an incompetent worker. He will recognize himself as inferior to all not only by his words—God will place in his heart an intimate feeling of this state. The monk will finally endeavor to do nothing except what is commended by the common rule of the monastery or the example of the seniors.

Chapter 71 marks a new summit of obedience. It is not only the abbot that the brothers are to obey but also one another, "convinced that it is by this way of obedience that they go to God." And, in the following chapter: "They earnestly compete with one another in obedience." Behind the "humble charity" of chapter 72 there stands the image of the monk entirely given to God and to his brothers, in a continual exercise of self-effacement and humble tenderness.

Such a grace of obedience exhibits all the aspects of the charism. It is a paschal situation since it renews in our midst the most characteristic attitude of Christ at the time of his return to the Father, his obedience unto death. Every Christian is called to reproduce this attitude, but some have received the gift to express it with a particular urgency in choosing a state of submission to others. Cenobitic life is rich in opportunities to live this grace. A superior is always at hand, as well the brothers who expect self-effacement and docility. One thus applies oneself to obedience all the day long. This is the humble love that Saint Benedict expects of the monk in regard to his abbot, the fervent zeal thanks to which he forgets himself without ceasing and anticipates all the other brothers in showing honor.[6] There is thus a grace of the hidden life which is proper to monastic life. No doubt this is the reason why Saint Benedict manifests a certain reticence with regard to monks being ordained to the priesthood. Every upward movement goes contrary to this fundamental aspiration of the monk.[7]

---

[6] See RB 72.3.
[7] See RB 62.

One last question concerns the link between the charism of spiritual obedience and the obedience which we have called social. The two types of obedience merge in the concrete, since the superior before whom the monk seeks to efface himself is at the same time the one responsible for the common good of the group. But the points of view remain different. The charge of the common good is a responsibility shared fraternally with all the brothers. The grace of silent self-effacement is a personal charism and, in a sense, exceptional. This grace does not need a superior responsible for the common good in order to be exercised. According to Benedict, one effaces oneself before all the brothers, before everyone. And the abbot himself is not dispensed from this. Jesus has shown him how all evangelical authority is a service of self-abasement that does not find itself at ease except in the last place.

Obedience as Docility (or Discernment)

In the self-abasement of Christ, obedience already appears to us as a paschal trajectory. It presupposes therefore a death and a resurrection. According to Saint John Climacus, "obedience buries the will and brings humility to life." The object of crucifixion and mortification, through the trial of obedience, is thus specified: it is the *will*, or indeed *self-will*, or even, in the plural, *willful desires*.

Clarifications of vocabulary immediately become necessary. What did the early monastic fathers understand by this *will* that they attack with such ardor? "Someone asked Abba Ammonas, 'What is the straight and narrow way?' He responded: 'To do violence to one's thoughts and to cut off one's own will for the sake of God.'"[8] Saint John Cassian is not any softer when he describes the first principles necessary to inculcate in the young novice: "The concern and the principal object of the teaching of the father . . . will be to teach [the novice] first of all to conquer his own will."[9] And Saint Benedict himself, for all his discretion,

---

[8] *Sayings*, Ammonas 5.
[9] J. Cassien, *Institutions cénobitiques* 4.8, SC 109 (Paris: Éditions du Cerf, 2001).

shows himself almost violent when he commands his monks simply to "hate self-will."[10]

In these texts, the will is obviously not understood as the spiritual faculty that loves or as the source of freedom and self-gift. No one is being asked to eliminate within himself the deep dynamism of personhood. To the contrary, the cutting off of self-will aims at the enhancement of freedom, but a freedom in harmony with the truth of the human being.

In the writings of the early monastic fathers, "the will" connotes rather whims and desires still emerging in their riotous state, unexamined and not yet discerned according to love. These multiple attractions can be affected by what remains of the dynamic of sin in us, even after the grace of baptism. If we are not on our guard, these enticements can incline us to illusion and sin, for these desires abound within us in a relatively exterior zone, peripheral in relation to the depths of our being. They lack the *simplicity* that existed before sin. Where they manifest themselves, they threaten to irritate existing wounds. Sometimes they even succeed in monopolizing to their own advantage our most profound liberty that, disoriented by them, then becomes what a certain ascetical vocabulary calls, not without reason, *self-will*.

The early monastic fathers had experience of the way in which the life of the Spirit generally makes a path for itself within us. They knew how to distinguish two states in the human person. The first can be identified by a term of ancient usage: namely, the state of *simplicity* (2 Cor 11:3). This is the state toward which we tend, wherein our being will be wholly restored by grace. All the fancies of the human person will then be unified and appeased by love.

The other state is that of the *multiplicity of desires*. This is the only condition we really know. We are conscious of a bundle of desires that to a large extent elude us and drag us along by all the senses, tossing us about on the restless waves of impressions and instincts. These superficial desires distract us from our interior life and scatter us outside ourselves, veiling within us the

[10] See RB 4.60.

fundamental desire that we bear which is the desire for God, placed in our heart by the Holy Spirit.

At the heart of this state of distraction we see confirmed the celebrated apophthegm of Abba Poemen: "Self-will is a wall of bronze between God and man."[11] To be reunited with God, only one means commends itself if we expand on the image suggested by Abba Poemen: tearing down the wall of self-will. The young monk will therefore learn to renounce all the desires that keep him far from his own deep self and from the desire for God within him. Once these desires have been removed, the monk finds himself again stripped of all self-willing, in an interior void where he avoids attaching himself to anything whatsoever. It is then that the desire for God, planted within his heart, will normally and, as it were, spontaneously rise to the surface.

Several parallel examples among non-Christian techniques of recollection immediately suggest themselves. But it is not necessary to go searching so far afield. In the New Testament itself one perceives the conviction according to which the renunciation of desire constitutes a properly Christian approach to therapy. The teaching can be paraphrased as follows: "Renounce your desire, whatever it may be, and when you have done so, the desire for God and rejoicing in him will rise up in your heart" (cf. 1 Pet 4:1-3; 1 John 2:16-17; John 1:13).

Jesus Christ was the first to emerge victorious in the struggle within him between two desires, and in the effacement of self-seeking human desire before the desire for God. He died of this victory. He was the first man in whom the desire *for* and the will *of* God were able to manifest themselves fully. Not only did he accomplish God's will perfectly, but he also became the man in whom the will of God made its home, the man totally identified with the divine will. Maybe this is the meaning that one must attribute to those words pronounced by the Father: "This is my Beloved Son, in him I have placed all my love" (Matt 3:17). Christ's obedience is the necessary corollary here below of that love of the Father that envelops the Son at the heart of

---

[11] *Sayings*, Poemen 48.

the Trinity. Obedience is thus a synonym for love. It is already inscribed in the trinitarian dynamic. Jesus himself makes this known to us: "If the Father loves me, it is because I give my life" (John 10:17).

This communion of wills between the Father and the Son does not come automatically for Jesus. During the agony of Gethsemane and on the cross, Jesus will be compelled to wrest this union from a terrible struggle. According to the text of Saint Luke, he enters into agony (Luke 22:44) and finds it necessary to pray that he might be in a position to give free rein to God's will within his own heart: "Not my will, but yours be done" (Luke 22:42). At a given moment Jesus will feel abandoned by his Father. This will be the crux of the crisis. But a few instants later, at the moment of death, he will at length give the perfect response to the declaration pronounced over him by the Father at the moment of his baptism. He expires handing over his spirit into the Father's hands: "Father, into your hands I commend my spirit" (Luke 23:46; NAB). It is love that is then exhaled in the restored communion of obedience.

After the example of Christ, the monk curtails his self-will so that the will of God may be fully revealed in him and may restore in him the totality of his paschal being. The retrenchment of desires fosters the surging of the freedom of a being made new in Jesus Christ. Obedience thus becomes a veritable spiritual therapy: by progressively reducing the interior dispersion of untamed desires, obedience liberates the human person and sets her on the path to her renewed humanity.

This way of freedom cannot be dissociated from the opening of the heart and the discernment that this opening initiates. We find ourselves here before one of the fundamental practices of the monastic tradition, but this is not the place to discuss it. Let's simply note that it is always in the light of another's regard that the disciple learns progressively to discern his desires and to cut off those that are evil. He is progressively set free of the dark forces that inhabit and paralyze him. He extricates himself from the false guilt that held him at its mercy in shame and fear. The welcome given him by his spiritual father dissipates this shadow and lightens its weight. The monk can finally discern where sin is truly to be found. Reconciled with his desires, he can recognize those that correspond to the true depth of his being and which he can engage in his whole life. But, at the same time, he becomes capable of renouncing other desires without superfluous trauma. In the deepest sense of the word, he is now *free* for obedience.

What is the connection between this obedience of discernment and social obedience? The spiritual father no doubt plays an important role here. But he is not necessarily the authority of the monastic group, and the service rendered by him does not aim, in the first instance, at the common good. To the contrary, the tie that binds the monk to his spiritual father is much more personal than that which obtains between himself and his superiors. The former presupposes a reciprocal trust, and the experience that one draws from it generally remains unique and capable of exerting its influence over long years of monastic life.

Even today, the abbot is rarely the spiritual father of each one of his monks. It remains true, however, that in a monastic climate, the obedience expected by the superior will always be pregnant with the therapeutic grace that is proper to obedience-as-discernment. Without forgetting the common good, it puts the emphasis on the personal welfare of each brother. For it is principally through obedience that the monk makes his way to God.[12]

Prophetic Obedience

The mystery of obedience is related to that of prophecy. When God suddenly intervenes in history to make his Word known, the human person is then absolutely sure to grasp, through the mouth of the prophet, the will of God. Certain characteristics of prophecy appear also in monastic obedience as we have just described it. Such obedience thus becomes a prophetic domain. The will of God is revealed through it, beyond any doubt, to the one who believes in it and obeys. Saint Benedict strongly underscores this

---

[12] See RB 71.2.

trait, but he is thereby only continuing a long tradition: the monk must obey "as if the order came from God himself."[13]

The adjective "prophetic" could be changed to "apostolic," since spiritual obedience inserts us as disciples into the lineage of the apostles and their successors. It is in this sense that Saint Benedict, following the Master, applies to those who exercise authority within the monastery the words that Jesus addressed to his apostles: "Whoever hears you, hears me" (Luke 10:16). Within the practice of obedience, the Word of God makes itself present with absolute certainty.

But it is important to be precise. This infallibility of obedience does not come first of all from the superior. It derives rather from the faith and the humility of the one who sincerely seeks God's will. Even if we can speak of a "grace of state," this grace does not belong in the first instance to the one who commands but rather to the one who obeys. The one who seeks with faith can never lack the manifestation of God's will: "If someone directs his heart to the divine will, God will illuminate even a little child to make him recognize it. If someone, on the contrary, does not seek the divine will sincerely and yet goes to consult a prophet, God will put into the heart of the prophet a response conforming to the perversity of the seeker's heart."[14]

Obedience provokes a prophetic miracle, so to speak. It suffices that there be a convergence of spiritual conditions for this miracle to burst forth: humility, openness of heart before the elder, sincere effort to curtail one's personal desires, search in faith for the will of the Lord. In such a case, God does not resist. He intervenes without fail, his will manifests itself in a striking way, and the one who thus delivers himself up to obedience is sure to conform himself to the will of God.

---

[13] See RB 5.4.

[14] Dorotheos of Gaza, *Instructions* 5.68, *Œuvres Spirituelles*, ed. and trans. L. Régnault and J. de Préville (Paris: Éditions du Cerf, 1963).

Cenobitic Obedience

Up until now we have underlined those aspects of an obedience defined as "spiritual" or "charismatic" to distinguish it from "social obedience." This discernment was essential to our project. But when the mystery of obedience is lived out communally, a new dimension appears which is also very important: that of the fraternal group. This latter is not merely social; it represents the Body of Christ. Saint Benedict calls the monastic community a *congregatio*, a term that the Latin Bible reserves for the assembly of the People of God in the desert. Now, at the head of this community, we inevitably find the leader, himself also a symbol of the Head of the Body and therefore of Christ in person.

This group of brothers has a real stability. Saint Benedict calls it "the battle line of the ranks of the brothers" from which one may not absent oneself without an exceptional vocation.[15] To be separated from it by excommunication is the gravest penalty in the Rule.[16] There exists a "body of the monastery," into which the newcomer is not integrated until the moment of his definitive commitment.[17] There is also a "stability in the congregation," which Saint Benedict identifies as the distinctive mark of his monks.[18] These latter belong to a corps of brothers who, all of them together, are conduits to Christ.[19] This corps represents, in a certain manner, the Church.

The group is, in addition, thoroughly structured: it has its form of life relatively separated from the world, its own schedule, common objectives, liturgy, rhythm of life, ritual of admission, and penal code. It possesses a superior charged with establishing the cohesion of the group and with orienting all the members toward the common good.

Social obedience inevitably comes into play here but remains of a particular type. If the monastic group—we could say the

---

[15] See RB 1.
[16] See RB 23.4.
[17] See RB 58.23.
[18] See RB 4.78.
[19] See RB 72.11.

monastic *Church*—possesses a hierarchy of its own, such a hierarchy relates most originally to the ecclesiastical authority. No doubt the bishops of the environs have the right to oversee what happens in the interior of the monastery, as do the abbots of the region besides,[20] for the little monastic "Church" lives in communion with the great universal Church. It possesses, however, its own spiritual consistency. It embraces the principle of succession for the authority that is exercised within the community. The abbots are not named by the bishops, but there is a succession among them, whether they be designated by the predecessor, as in the Rule of the Master, or elected by the community itself, or by the best of the monks, as envisioned by Saint Benedict.

If he is elected by his brothers, the abbot nevertheless does not receive his charge from their hands. In the midst of his brothers, he first of all holds the place of the Lord. Being vicar of Christ according to Saint Benedict, he bears this name in addition to those of pastor, father of a family, steward of the house of God, and servant of the Lord, chosen to distribute the grain at the proper time.[21] His is a difficult and arduous task: to govern souls and to adapt himself to the dispositions of each one. On the Day of Judgment, the Lord will demand an account for all of them as well as for himself.[22]

At the heart of the monastic Church, the grace of state commanding obedience will not be located only or even principally in the disciple, as was the case in the prophetic obedience studied above. It will be first of all centered in the leader.

Cenobitic obedience is the place toward which the diverse aspects of the charism of obedience, examined in the foregoing, come to converge. As they unceasingly blend together, they unite in the experience of a bond with concrete authority and an obedience of which the sociological components are fully respected.

Cenobitic obedience, however, remains marked above all by the charism. It expresses the internal cohesion that the commu-

---

[20] See RB 69.4-6.
[21] See RB 64.21.
[22] See RB 2.37-38.

nity fundamentally *is*, whatever the social pressures that make themselves felt at its heart. The authority is at the service of this cohesion. All the aspects of charismatic obedience find themselves contained and recapitulated in the common good of this community of monks united by the love of Christ and in the patrimony that is there transmitted. This common good, along with celibacy, ascesis, and prayer, is the *bonum oboedientiae*, the "good of obedience," as it is called by Saint Benedict.[23] It is a charism of self-abasement, of discernment of the will of God through the complete renunciation of one's own desire, for the abbot as much as for the brothers. If social obedience necessarily exists at the heart of the monastic group, it has no other goal but to guarantee the full flowering of this charism. Indeed, Saint Benedict holds the abbot responsible not only for the orders that he gives but also for the obedience of his disciples.[24] Monastic authority is at the service of the charism of each of the monks.

---

[23] See RB 71.1.
[24] See RB 2.37-38.

6

Apostolic and Contemplative Dimensions of Religious Life

Should We Distinguish between "Contemplative" and "Active" Religious?

My own spiritual experience was born and has grown within the context of monastic life, which at certain times has also (somewhat uncritically) been called "contemplative" life. But does this mean that my personal witness to the consecrated life must therefore be vastly different from the one given by a religious living what is called the "apostolic" life? Of course the exterior form, the field of action, the rhythm of life, can be notably different in each case, but surely these differences are but signs of an interior experience that develops on the level of the life of faith, itself common to all the baptized. Giving witness to the value of the consecrated life should therefore not be the occasion for making a fundamental distinction between those who, seen from the outside, can be catalogued and distinguished as "active" and "contemplative" religious. Does there not somewhere have to be an *a priori* common ground, a shared source for both forms of consecrated life?

By naively posing this question at the very start, I am aware of having already put my cards on the table so as to reveal the tenor of what will follow. In fact, the more one plumbs the experience of a believer, the more one tries to grasp somewhat this mysterious life called "spiritual" or "interior." But when our subject is the very life of God and his breath moving deep in our being, we should take great care that our choice of words not be haphazard or derive from an old-fashioned vocabulary repeated by rote. The more one tries to grasp God's life in us, the more there is a blurring and even a vanishing of the borders that a certain convenient language would cause us to draw between two ways of life, or rather between two intense periods of the same experience: namely, active life and contemplative life.

At bottom, as I bear witness before you today, it is this that my heart most impels me to say to you and which will also lead me to go beyond the boundaries of the contemplative framework, where "contemplative" is used in the strict sense, in order to sum up the whole of the religious life such as I encounter it at the heart of my own monastic vocation.

In the course of your ministry to consecrated religious, have you never sensed the feeling of irritation or annoyance that most "contemplatives" feel when one wants to decorate them with this title? This unease cannot be explained only in terms of the ending of a certain triumphalism of the "better part," now largely recognized as obsolete in the Church. Nor does it express a sort of fashionable defiance against the term "contemplative," suspected of Neoplatonism by a portion of the intelligentsia, even among believers. Contemplative religious are generally too down-to-earth to pay attention to such quibbles. No, they believe profoundly in their way of life as well as in contemplation, in the most ancient sense of the term. But they feel ill at ease when someone attempts to define the whole of their life by what constitutes only one single dimension—fundamental and important, certainly, but which they nonetheless experience as something fragile; I would almost say precarious. It is not at all a reality that is theirs to manage since it is pure grace. Who would dare to introduce oneself as a "contemplative" or a specialist in contemplation? It does not belong exclusively to them; for surely there are more contemplatives to be found outside of monasteries than within them. Finally, there is the risk that such an emphasis may eclipse other, no less important aspects of their experience as believers.

This unease of contemplatives before the title that others bestow on them explains in its own way how the distinction between contemplative and active lives, from the viewpoint of daily experience, is not entirely adequate. Perhaps the two converge on a common ground that will be important for us to explore.

Contemplatives in Canon Law

The distinction between "active" and "contemplative" remains useful, however. I would not want to dispense with it altogether. This is all the more the case since, contrary to the 1917 Code of Canon Law, the new Code of 1983 officially canonizes, after the pattern of the council, the fact that a certain kind of religious life is "totally *ordered to the contemplative life*." Of course, a code of law cannot be concerned with "contemplation" in the theological sense of the word, since in this realm, law by definition can have no purchase; but the Code does address so-called "canonical" contemplative life, something that the law can and sometimes must regulate in certain ways.

That the new Code is concerned to do so gives me cause for rejoicing. Law exists neither to restrain nor to oppress. Its primary function is to liberate, to make possible, to favor what something ought to be, and thus to ensure protection against all that could ruin it. It is normal that the Code should specify those conditions under which a religious life that claims to be contemplative may indeed be so fully, within the structures of the Church.

Let us pause for a moment to linger, if you will, on the canons that treat of this subject and note that here we encounter one of the constants not only of the so-called contemplative life but also, I believe, of all religious life.

If I am not mistaken, the mention of institutes "wholly ordered to the contemplative life" appears twice in the new Code. First there is canon 667, which treats of enclosure. Enclosure, it is important to note, is demanded of all forms of religious life; it will simply be stricter in monasteries of contemplative life. Again, where contemplative nuns are concerned, such enclosure will be papal, that is to say that its norms will be specified or approved by the Holy See itself. Here we find already one of the constants of all religious life, but one that is particularly set in relief by contemplatives: all religious begin by making a certain withdrawal from the world. The religious represents that aspect of the Church that must remain oriented to the desert.

The second mention of religious institutes entirely ordered to the contemplative life appears in the following section devoted to the apostolate of religious. It is located in canon 674, a very dense canon whose theological inspiration and even literary sources derive from several conciliar documents:

> Institutes which are wholly ordered to contemplation always retain a distinguished position in the mystical Body of Christ: for they offer an extraordinary sacrifice of praise to God, they illuminate the people of God with the richest fruits of their sanctity, they move it by their example, and extend it through their hidden apostolic fruitfulness. For this reason, however much the needs of the active apostolate demand it, members of these institutes cannot be summoned to aid in various pastoral ministries.[1]

This second canon concerns the specifically apostolic character of the contemplative life, an apostolicity considered particular and mysterious, linked in fact to the desert, symbolized by a withdrawal, and by the cloister for which the Church demands continued respect.

These two canons furnish us with the two parts of this conference: first, the desert and what is supposed to occur there; then the apostolic fruitfulness that springs up from it, mysteriously to be sure, as the law says of it, but also according to certain criteria that may be equally verified elsewhere in the Church, according to a dynamic that expresses what is no doubt the deepest but also the most common of Christian experiences.

A Church Formed in the Desert

The call to the desert is inscribed in the heart of the Church. Not in the form of nostalgia for a glorious past but as the sole

---

[1] *Code of Canon Law*, Latin-English Edition (Washington, DC: Canon Law Society of America, 1983), 255.

condition for a future in which God will always continue to be powerfully at work. The desert is a fundamental theological structure of the Church which, before the return of Jesus at the end of time, can never be rendered void.

And that has always been so. The desert is the place where the Church is born and grows. In Abraham, called to a nomadic existence, in Moses and the people delivered from Egypt, launched upon the ways of an interminable exodus, from desert to desert, the People of God have progressed down the ages. The desert remains burned into its memory, it inhabits its reminiscences, it haunts its plans. At every juncture of salvation history, Jews have been impelled into the desert to relive the Passover and there to prepare for a new passing-over. Jesus, in his turn, irresistibly, at the moment of his mission's inauguration, is led by the Spirit of God into solitude, as have been all the Fathers who knew by experience that the ways of God are prepared in the desert and that the fruits of the Spirit are there conceived.

The Church also remains forever oriented toward the desert, even today. There she sinks down her roots as if in a territory of God, in the maternal soil of the exodus and the Passover. There she has her lines of communication that enable her to function. She does not hesitate to come away and withdraw there, at certain times, to gain some distance and to recollect herself for a moment so as to bring to maturity the words that she will announce to people all the more vigorously for having first heard them from the mouth of God. The Church can appear marginal, can provoke astonishment, can even evoke hatred, the hatred found in the gospels and that Jesus promises to his Church on the part of the world. But she can never doubt that her relevance is tied to the desert of the prophets and of Jesus, where she is unceasingly convoked to take her full measure and her consistency.

You see already that this spirit of the desert, which should never be foreign to any Christian vocation, is taken up as the responsibility, in a more significant way, by religious life and, in a manner still more urgent, by a tradition that goes back to the earliest times of the Church: the tradition of monks and of those we call contemplatives.

But what is it all for? What happens in the desert? Does anything happen in the desert? Indeed, it is important that something happen there, that something befall the one who retires there. We would be speaking too casually of the Christian desert if we only compared it to a refuge where one can take shelter from certain dangers, or even to see it—which has been done—as a greenhouse whose special conditions permit the growth and maturation of spiritual flowers and fruits. One does not go to the desert for tranquility, to enjoy a certain peace that is supposed to facilitate what one hopes to be a life of intimacy with God. These images are too lyrical, bespeaking a certain laziness. They are frankly insufficient to describe the desert Christian.

Neither shelter, nor refuge, nor hothouse, the desert is rather a crucible where, thanks to a certain fire—simultaneously that of the passions and that of the Holy Spirit—a noble metal will emerge, purified of its dross, or a new alloy will see the light of day—daring, novel, and unknown until the present. Or, to employ an image that is at once biological and biblical, the desert is a womb where, in the inevitable pangs of birth, a new being comes into the light, the new man created in Jesus Christ in justice and holiness.

I find a more modern definition for the desert of religious life in the title of a book written by a famous American psychiatrist and devoted to psychiatric hospitals: *A Place of Rebirth*. This is also the definition of the Church and, at the same time, of every religious community.

But what sort of birth or rebirth is envisioned here? This new being will be a being of communion, in a double sense: fraternal communion and communion with God.

First, I would like to offer a brief word on fraternal communion, because then I will speak at some length on the other sort.[2] God does not doom anyone to remain solitary, not even the hermit—perhaps above all not the hermit, who is called to become a communal being of the first rank, according to the celebrated formula of Evagrius Ponticus, "separated from all and united to all." God

---

[2] See A. Louf, "Living in a Fraternal Community," chap. 4 of the present book, p. 32–34.

calls each of us to a community, to a concrete Church, even in the desert. It is in the desert, according to the witness of the Bible, that the first *qahal-ekklesia* was constituted. *Qahal-ekklesia* is rendered in the Latin Vulgate as *congregatio*, and Saint Benedict will apply this term to the monastic community. Through him, *congregatio* will know a rich and long development since even today the term forms part of the normal vocabulary of religious life.

I will content myself with calling your attention to the admirable canon 602 which, in the new Code, follows immediately after the canons dealing with the three evangelical counsels of obedience, poverty, and chastity. The legislator wanted to devote this privileged place to fraternal life:

> The life of the brothers or sisters (*vita fraterna*) proper to each institute, by which all the members are united together like a special family in Christ, is to be determined in such a way that it becomes a mutual support for all in fulfilling the vocation of each member. Moreover, by their communion as brothers or sisters (*fraterna communione*), rooted in and built on love, the members are to be an example of universal reconciliation in Christ.[3]

One of the principal instances in which religious life gives witness to itself is that of the reconciliation that Christ works among brothers of one and the same Church. Simply on this basis, prior to offering a message or performing any works, the life is apostolic. It signifies and realizes the Church.

But this reconciliation presupposes yet another: that of each brother with the Lord, in an encounter for which the desert offers a particularly apt terrain and, indeed, the most appropriate place since it is the theological landscape through which God chose to lead his people in order to give himself to them.

A Place of Poverty

But why the desert? Not because it makes things easier by removing a certain number of distracting obstacles—I have already

---

[3] *Code of Canon Law*, Latin-English Edition, 227.

hinted at this—but because the desert is called on to provoke the crisis and, so to speak, to force the event that God wishes to make happen to each of his children.

How does the desert provoke the event? The Bible describes the desert as a "dry land, thirsty and without water" (Ps 62:1). The one who ventures there, always led by the Spirit of God and not by his own audacity, is generally unaware of the sort of trial to which he thus exposes himself. The honeymoon there is of very short duration. Soon there remains only desolation, loneliness, the lack of provisions and of earthly foods, and, at the same time, the leaden sky, the arid sand or—in the Nordic deserts—the impenetrable fog and the depressing drizzle. God hides himself, sometimes for days or years. But above all, the human being himself succumbs to lassitude or discouragement and sometimes collapses, constrained as he is to live like one reduced to an extreme, meeting day after day with the poignant experience of his own poverty, weakness, radical powerlessness, and evident uselessness, beyond anything he had supposed.

Many and various are the places where this weakness can manifest itself in me, but the fact is that it always manifests itself—such is the tactic and the holy ruse of God—precisely where I am at my most vulnerable, stripped of my defenses, where I am totally diminished to an almost fatal extreme of weakness, where there remains but one single hope: that of finally laying down my arms and capitulating before God, that is to say, the hope of exposing myself, of casting myself upon his mercy, of allowing myself to be retrieved by grace at the place and at the precise moment where I was on the point of foundering.

I am not exaggerating in thus describing the crisis provoked by the desert that serves as a prelude to the event. I am weighing each of my words. It would be easy to illustrate it by numerous passages borrowed from the most ancient monastic literature which, alas, is still too often viewed as suspect of extreme willful asceticism. In actual fact, this literature offers the most admirable and ancient pages on what we now call "spiritual poverty" or "childhood."

All these humble ascetical efforts, far from being the accomplishments that a spiritual athlete wishes to parade, have but one goal: to break the heart of the one who risks engaging in them. "Breaking the heart" (*diatribê tês kardias* or *contritio cordis*) is a phrase of ancient origin. What does it mean? Through the experience of the desert, the neophyte ascetic is brought progressively to the conviction that the life he wanted to lead entirely exceeds his strength. To begin with, there is sexual continence, then also vigils, fasting, and work, but not without the fraternal life and the support of others. Left to himself, the ascetic is radically incapable of all that. God comes to shatter the mirror of his ideal of perfection at which he liked now and then to cast a furtive glance. But above all, God has broken his heart. He is reduced to an extreme and he finds no exit from his plight.

This crisis will affect equally, and perhaps even particularly, his prayer, from which he expected so much, as well as his faith. Before it turns into jubilation, prayer itself passes through a desert where God is apparently absent but which is the obligatory vestibule of all Christian contemplation. It would be futile to look for a shortcut. There is no fast track for attaining to God, nor prayer without pain, without waiting, without a humble patience that does not quit. This hollowing out can extend very far and can unveil those monsters in our inner depths that we would have preferred not to awaken. In prayer, even of the least persevering sort, the Church and above all the contemplative find themselves confronted by their share of atheism, not the atheism of the unbelievers but the kind that each one of us painfully carries deep inside us. As curious as it may seem, before becoming an expert in the things of God, the monk is first an expert in atheism. He finds himself fraternally joined to all those who doubt and who have not yet succeeded in abandoning themselves to the tenderness of God. The monk knows by experience what this crucible of faith is and how the hand of God works through it, stripping us of all our idols. In the person of the contemplative confronted by his night, the Church accepts the trial of faith in all its magnitude.

This trial of the desert is one which other spiritual masters describe through different images, such as "cloud" or "night," but all these images point to the same spiritual experience. It reaches down to the very roots of the human person, uncovering wounds of the personality so sensitive and defenseless that, from a human point of view, he seems to touch in passing the edge of mental imbalance, the type of madness that has power over him within his psyche. Evagrius, the great master of the desert, analyzes in detail certain manifestations of this famous *acedia*, and these strangely approximate the symptoms of the interior collapse that today we very modestly refer to as "nervous depression."

The help of an expert guide is, therefore, surely necessary to verify at each instant that it is still the Holy Spirit leading into such straits; but there is no cause for surprise, much less for taking fright. For salvation is always at hand. More than ever, God will save. Reduced to the extremity of our weakness, we are finally mature enough to be set free, to be restored by a merciful and infinitely powerful grace.

A Place of Rebirth

God's hands, you see, are now free to work, and his achievement is always a miracle, the marvel of the new humanity, re-created in Jesus Christ. In his *Life of Saint Antony*, Saint Athanasius describes in detail and at length the horror of the temptations that the father of monks had to suffer until the day when God intervened in his favor. For long years hidden away in the tomb that afforded him solitude, Antony at last emerges and presents himself to the astonished crowd. And we are struck by how the bishop of Alexandria depicts, in a slightly tremulous style touched with lyricism, this new man who held fast on the threshold of his desert. We should listen to him with some humor, and this in no way impairs the density of the vocabulary employed:

> The appearance of Antony remained the same; he had neither grown fat for lack of physical exercise, nor emaciated by fasting and combat with demons, but he was just such as he had been known before his withdrawal. His soul was pure, neither shrunken by bitterness, nor softened through pleasure; in him neither excess, nor turmoil; the crowd did not trouble him, nor did he take excessive joy at being greeted by such a great number of persons; always the same within himself,

under the guidance of the Spirit, he remained unmoved in the
splendor of his nature.[4]

I have only paraphrased slightly in translating the final term
of the last sentence (*en tô kata physin*), inasmuch as "nature," for
the Greek Fathers, is the new humanity, the human being restored
to what he was before the fall and on his way to attaining the
plenitude of humanity in Jesus Christ. There can be no doubt
that, behind the description of certain traits that could nowadays
astonish us, this is indeed what Athanasius is trying to say to us.
For Antony, the desert was a place where one could be reborn.
The tomb of solitude has become the paschal tomb of Christ,
with whom Antony has just been raised up. In following Christ,
the man of God is purely and simply humanity in the splendor
of its nature, according to God's design.

But at the price of what great trials! And so this new being
must be described not so much with the philosophical vocabulary
in which Athanasius allows himself to indulge only a bit, but
rather, with the aid of a soteriological vocabulary, the vocabulary
of salvation. Here mention is always made of sin forgiven, blindness healed, and wounds and scars that will always remain, no
less on the ascetic than those on the body of Jesus, but henceforth
in order to attest to the victory of God and his grace.

The ascesis of the contemplative—and all Christian ascesis—
thus has first of all to do with poverty, the training in poverty of
the poor person who will never cease to be such even if, one day,
having completed this decisive pass-over, he finds himself finally
and completely at peace, having been unmade and remade from
the bottom up by pure grace. He has crossed the abyss of mercy.
He has learned to surrender to God, to take off his mask, and
to lay down his arms. He has found himself bereft before God,
no longer disposed in any way to defend himself against divine
love. He is truly stripped naked. He has been dispossessed of
his virtues, his plans, and his health. He retains nothing except
his laborious misery, in order to spread it out before Mercy. God

---

[4] Athanasius, *Life of Saint Antony* 14.

has truly become God for him, and God alone, that is to say the savior from his sin. At length he is able to make peace even with his sin, to rejoice in his weakness. He is henceforth uninterested in his own perfection: it is nothing but dirty laundry in the eyes of God (cf. Isa 54:6). He possesses his virtues only within: they are his wounds, now dressed and healed by mercy. He can do nothing but give glory to God who works within him and continues unceasingly to work marvels.

Among his brothers also he is a new man, that is, a tender and gentle friend who is not irritated by others' faults and who is understanding of weaknesses. He would be the first to distrust himself infinitely and to betray a mad confidence in God, relying totally on his mercy and omnipotence.

Does he now contemplate something more precise in God? Does he from now on know him better? If one asked him the question in this way, he would be at a loss to respond or, probably, he would respond in the negative. He still has the impression of being plunged in the same dark night. Yet something has changed in him. A new sensibility has progressively emerged. A strange presentiment inhabits him. He knows neither God nor Christ, but he sometimes surprises himself by divining them, by nearly recognizing them, by savoring a presence not only while at prayer or while ruminating the Word of God but also elsewhere, in faces that are suffering or joyful, in the unfolding of events in which he now discerns a course and a design. He not only knows now why he must, at certain hours, extend his prayer for a lengthy period, but he also begins to sense as if by instinct what he must do or say at other times, how he must behave. For he no longer flies with his own wings, nor at his own risk or to his own peril. He is borne aloft on the wings of another. He is, as it were, impelled from within. He discovers that he is mysteriously led: "Those who are led by the Spirit are truly sons of God" (Rom 8:14). He need only allow it to happen. Another is at work within him. Another is working wonders there. And he perceives, in the very depths of his being, that barely perceptible call, like a murmur of incessant prayer, like an unction—as Saint John says (1 John 2:27)—that teaches him from day to day what he must do.

A Place that Attracts the Crowd

In trying to describe to you a little of this new man—who could be either contemplative or active—who is born in the desert, I have already advanced very far, you will have noticed, into the second part of my subject: the apostolic dimension of religious life. There is nothing surprising in this, since this aspect is inseparable from the first. Why was it that one day Saint Antony decided without any apparent hesitation to come out from his reclusion and break his silence? Simply because there was a crowd outside the door. A crowd of people who had come from afar and who were crying out noisily for a word from this hermit who until then had been living as if already buried. And behold, we find ourselves, perhaps for the first time, before a phenomenon that is going to repeat itself indefinitely throughout the entire history of monastic and religious life and that illustrates splendidly the inescapable correlation between the contemplative and the active lives and the interior dynamism that one lends the other. In most cases, the contemplative does not take up the mission and vocation to leave the desert and proclaim the Word to others. In ancient monastic literature, such a desire is denounced as a temptation of the evil one. On the contrary, it is the People of God itself that recognizes the one who has received the Word on its behalf, who leaves the city to lay siege to the desert, if one may put it thus, and to force open the doors of the enclosure.

In this way there is established in the heart of the Church a continual give-and-take between the desert and the city. The monk seems to flee the city, but scarcely has he gone to the edge of the desert, scarcely has the latter began to bear some fruit, when the city hastens to go out from itself to flee to the monk, to follow his steps, to beg him for a word, and to clamor for his blessing.

This phenomenon, verified so many times in the course of history even to this day, reminds the monk of two things: first, the essential importance of the desert stage in every religious life, whether contemplative or apostolic. Only one transformed by the desert, only the "new man," can become the tested lover who irresistibly attracts the People of God.

Again, this phenomenon reminds the monk that a place exists where the frontier between the desert and the world vanishes. Monks do not have to return to the world, and neither does the world have to withdraw to the desert. For there is a place where desert and world are no longer juxtaposed as alternatives. In a Saint Antony, in any man of God, the desert and the world coincide in a place called the Church. The Church is sent to the world, and yet she does not belong to the world. She does not dilute herself or conform herself to the world. In order to proclaim the Word, she can confront the world because she remains always oriented to the desert. So also is religious life with its double dimension, contemplative and apostolic.

What I still have to say on the more specifically apostolic dimension I will express from the standpoint of my own monastic experience. As for those who live a life that is strictly speaking "contemplative," I will attempt to sketch briefly how they feel themselves to be fully "apostolic."

A Place at the Heart of the Church

In my insistence on the necessary, dynamic overlap between contemplation and action in the one Christian existence, I could have given the impression of thinking that all contemplatives, after the pattern of an Antony or a Benedict, are called to leave their cloister one day in order to speak a word. But that is not at all my thinking. In fact, as is affirmed clearly by canon 674, cited at the beginning of this talk, there have at all times existed, and there exist still today, some contemplatives—monks and nuns—who are not called to share explicitly their experience with their brothers and sisters, and whom the Church intends to protect by her law from all unseasonable interference in a contrary direction. She does this, the canon says, in the name of a mysterious apostolic fruitfulness, inherent in the contemplative life, the authenticity of which the Church wishes to guarantee.

In every age these contemplative vocations have remained very discreet. Their exterior splendor, like that of the Virgin Mary, has been quantitatively negligible. Often it amounted to no more than a simple presence of extraordinary quality. In particular, our Latin Church has known, above all in the fourteenth and fifteenth centuries, a tradition of hermits and recluses in the strict sense of the word, a tradition that in the majority of cases—to judge by the literary vestiges that remain—was of real quality. There were equally some less admirable developments that explain a certain number of abuses and a rapid decline of that life up to the Council of Trent, which passed them over in silence in the official texts. Up to the present day, the canonical status of the hermit, recognized as forming part of the state of consecrated life, has yet to be restored by the new Code.

In what does this mysterious apostolic fruitfulness of the contemplative life consist? We think first of all of intercessory prayer, with which contemplatives feel themselves to be charged: "They pray"—as is sometimes said—"for those who do not pray." At the same time, one may take seriously their often explicit desire to "do penance for those who do not." But this remains insufficient, even if today we have at our disposal a more profound theology of intercession and of penance and reparation, than the previous, more negative model.

The same remark holds true for the function as role model that a community of contemplatives undoubtedly plays. But all of this—praying, doing penance, giving an example—is still of the order of action, whereas the fruitfulness proper to the contemplative life derives first of all from its being, from what has happened to the contemplative, from the enacted anthropology that was his Passover in the crucible of the desert, from the new man that he has become by pure grace. Without the contemplative's knowing how or why, this is what is important for salvation history today, so that the kingdom may arrive now. This is also the ultimate reason why his nightly or early-morning vigils take up the suspended waiting that slumbers in so many human hearts; the reason why his fasting expresses the hunger for God that tortures humanity unawares; the reason why his obedience is truly the Passion of Christ prolonging itself to this very day; and the reason why his celibacy, which he lives humbly and laboriously, progressively enlarges his heart to the utmost limits of the universe.

As a result of all this, the contemplative now loves in an entirely different way. Through the trial of the desert, his heart was broken; even better, it was melted. It has become the liquid heart of the saints, of which the Curé d'Ars spoke, a heart of stone transformed into a heart of flesh that embraces the entire universe and makes the contemplative a universal brother. He is no longer anything but kindness and mercy, in the image of that Mercy that he will one day meet face-to-face. And he knows by instinct how important it is, not only for himself but also for the universal Church, that he persevere in remaining where he is, in occupying this place that God has assigned to him. For he knows, well beyond his apparent uselessness, that at the heart of the Church, his Mother, he is love.

This conviction of mysteriously supporting the world does not date only from little Thérèse. It goes back to a remote epoch of monasticism, as is witnessed by this strange text of a Palestinian recluse of the sixth century to whom it had been revealed that the world of his times rested upon three extraordinary men of prayer:

> There are three men perfect in the sight of God . . . who have received the power to bind and to loose, to remit faults or to retain them. They stand fast in the breach to prevent the whole world from being annihilated at a single stroke and, thanks to their prayers, God will chastise with mercy. . . . The prayers of these three combine to gain access to the sublime altar of the Father of lights. They congratulate each other in a shared exaltation in the heavens. . . . These are John at Rome, Elias at Corinth, and another in the Eparchy of Jerusalem. And I am confident that they will obtain this great mercy. Yes, they will obtain it! Amen.[5]

A Place of Discernment

I now return to the apostolic life of religious called "active." I speak here of those who may be said to have gone through the

---

[5] Barsanuphe et Jean de Gaza, Letter 569, in *Correspondance* (Sablé-sur-Sarthe: Éditions de Solesmes, 1972), 369.

desert stage in one way or another. This experience, after transforming them, has given them rebirth into the world. I would then like to finish by saying something about spiritual discernment which is perhaps the essential grace of the new human being who has been restored in the desert.

Spiritual discernment is a grace that consists in a new sensitivity, a capacity of perceiving the invisible in the visible, in both contemplative and active experience. The perception of the Spirit's whispers within us as it cries out: "Abba, Father!," and the perception of this same Spirit's interior movement as it gently invites us to act: these two perceptions do not arise from two distinct spiritual organs. It is the same heart, keeping watch in a state of vigilance, that scrutinizes and listens at length, and to which it is granted to channel the interior action of the Holy Spirit, whether the Spirit is praying within us or whether he is inviting us to accomplish the will of the Father.

In the psychology of the new human being, this capacity to discern the Spirit is, in a certain sense, more important than the gift of prayer or the gift of apostolic action. These latter depend strictly on the movement of the Spirit and on the capacity of the subject correctly to register this movement. Whether one surrenders to the gift of prayer, or whether one allows oneself to be sent on a mission of apostolic witness, it is always thanks to the same Spirit. It is always by the same unction that one allows oneself to be led, as is said so admirably by Saint Bernard's first biographer when he writes of Bernard that he accomplished everything *unctione magistra*, that is, with the interior unction of the Holy Spirit as teacher and guide.

By contrast, nothing is more sterile or, in the end, more risky than to claim to have dedicated oneself to prayer, or to believe oneself sent to bear witness—however great may be the generosity thus deployed—if one is interiorly cut off from the Spirit and, if I may put it this way, incapable of allowing it to emerge within oneself or of perceiving it. All contemplative life and all active life would be thereby compromised.

One can thus understand in what sense Saint Ignatius claims to remain a "contemplative in action," he who had hesitated for long months between the cell of a Charterhouse and the Society he was to found. Not that he asks of his companions some sort of mental gymnastics that would oblige them to mix meditation with their apostolic concerns. He expects of them simply that, in the midst of service and action, they keep the interior ear attentive to the movement of the Spirit in the depths of the heart. The disciple of Ignatius—and one could say the same of every believer—speaks and acts as he listens to what is going on inside himself, paying attention to the movements of his heart. Echoing the whole monastic tradition, Ignatius thought that only the desire for God (or his will) would survive once the disciple had become indifferent to all his superficial desires, those that in most people encumber the soul and suffocate the desire for God. Is it not, however, this desire for God that founds and constitutes our most specific and richest identity?

According to Saint Ignatius, the examination of conscience must arrive at an understanding of the working of this same spiritual process. It goes far beyond what this exercise became afterward, under pressure from a willful moralism that transformed it into something like a balance sheet of sins and good deeds, tabulating profits and losses. The examination of conscience is simply a special moment of interior silence, of the desert rediscovered, that allows one to hear the beating of a heart in the state of vigil while faithfully taking note of the divine instinct of grace and the movements of the Holy Spirit within so as to adjust all human action to them. Is it thus so different from prayer, which likewise needs the same interior ear in order to unite itself with the groanings of the Spirit? The contemplative at prayer and the contemplative in action converge in this interior listening and looking, in this new sensitivity of the new humanity that the tradition calls *diakrisis* or discretion, spiritual discernment. This is an indispensable condition for the believer—whether praying or praising God or witnessing to him—to be able to remain connected to the very action of God.

Spiritual discernment is therefore like a common ground between the two dimensions (contemplative and active) of all religious life and all Christian life. These two dimensions take their origin from the same spiritual reality, given by an ear whose drum vibrates in unison with the least murmur of the Spirit, given as well by a gaze able to perceive the first rays of the Lord's presence. This is spiritual discernment. From their origins this has been the hidden treasure of monastic and religious life, in my conviction perhaps the most precious offering they can make to today's Church.

As we approach our conclusion, we come back to the question we asked when we began, on the distinction between the contemplative and the active life: "Must they not *a priori* have a common ground, a shared source?" It seems the answer is yes, indeed. By a different route we are ending up at the same source that the instruction on "The Contemplative Dimension of the Religious Life" indicated as a point of departure for all spiritual life: "The heart considered as the most intimate sanctuary of the person, in which vibrates the grace of the unity between interiority and activity."[6]

This same instruction recalled likewise that the principal goal of the formation of religious life was "to immerse the religious in the experience of God," so as to favor "the mutual penetration of interiority and activity, such that the conscience of each cultivates the priority of life in the Holy Spirit." In addition, it defined what we have called spiritual discernment in this way: "The more the religious opens himself to the contemplative dimension, the more he will make himself attentive to the demands of the kingdom, developing intensely his theological interiority, because he will observe events with the gaze of faith that will help him to discover everywhere the divine intention."

In fact, so long as the experience of the kingdom only touches the surface of our being, we experience the duality of the contemplative and active dimensions as a tearing apart and even, at the

---

[6] "The Contemplative Dimension of Religious Life," Plenaria of the Sacred Congregation for Religious and for Secular Institutes (March 4–7, 1980), par. 4, http://www.vatican.va/roman_curia/congregations/ccscrlife/documents/rc_con_ccscrlife_doc_12081980_the-contemplative-dimension-of-religious-life_en.html.

extreme, as an insurmountable dichotomy. But, in the measure that this same experience penetrates us on ever deeper levels, our apprehension of God and of his kingdom becomes simple and unified. At a certain depth of interiority, the paths of believers cannot be opposed, much less mutually exclusive. They grow ever closer to the point of resembling each other as two brothers. And therefore the better part belongs neither to one side nor the other. It is everywhere, it is the hidden treasure at the heart of each vocation.

7

In Solidarity

The question is asked of us: "How do you monks experience yourselves to be in solidarity with people and with the particular Churches?" The response calls for some nuances.

During these past few days, we have evoked some very concrete experiences of solidarity. The *solidarity* of monks indeed exists, but it is not entirely captured by what the term immediately suggests.

The question emerged also of a certain "distancing" by religious in relation to ecclesial structures. The monk himself, too, keeps a certain distance, but this does not coincide in all respects with the sorts of distance taking that have been evoked here.

We have often spoken of "particular Churches." Here, too, the monk does not take exception to the term. It alludes to his own experience. He even asks himself whether the type of life that he leads does not make him, up to a certain point, the sign of an ecclesial pluralism. At the same time, however, the very nature of his monastic project seems to exclude for him certain particularities that have been extolled. Allow me to explain.

Is the monk in solidarity with people and with the Churches? The humblest of monks, questioned on this subject, would without hesitation reply in the affirmative. One does not even have to search for this solidarity. It is a given from the very first. Even if, caught up in an illusion, such a monk dreamed of restoring a past century, he would still do so inevitably as a man of his time and of his generation. The only important thing here is to specify at what level of his humanity the monk seeks to experience and embody this solidarity.

The Hidden Man of the Heart

In order to respond to this question, I would like to invoke an old monastic saying. Saint Antony said that the solitary in the desert is spared three combats: that of the eyes, that of the tongue, and that of the ears. There remains for him only one battle: that of the heart.[1] All the same, I would readily assert that the monk's solidarity can, on several counts, liberate him the better to operate at the level of the heart.

The heart of a monk is the heart of man stripped naked, deprived of every contingency and having, in the midst of trial—and it matters little what sort of trial—the experience of his profound alienation and sin, of his immense need for God and of the power of God that re-creates him. It is this sort of man—who slumbers in the heart of every human being—that the monk seeks to encounter. His objective is not *homo faber*, the man of work who creates and produces, even though work has never been lacking in monastic institutes and though their insertion into the economic world poses very particular problems for monks. Nor is it *homo sapiens* the monk seeks, the man in search of knowledge, even though there has always been a monastic form of reflection and, it is claimed, of theology. Rather, what the monk looks for is, to borrow an expression from Saint Peter, *homo absconditus cordis*, the "hidden man of the heart" (1 Pet 3:4), the one who is confusedly religious, on the watch for transcendence, who spontaneously confronts today a society of comfort and ease in the name of a quest whose end cannot be hastened.

In Solitude

Paradoxically, the monk arrives at this solidarity of the heart in *solitude*, which here should not connote distance or absence. On the contrary, true solitude, of which the material cloister is but a minor symbol, lies at the very heart of the world and of humanity. It constitutes a dimension of the world and of the human heart.

[1] See *Sayings*, Antony 11.

One would take flight from it in vain. The most secret depths of the human person remain unexplored so long as he has not yet been brought to the very limit of his solitude.

Insofar as we are all in some sense unbelievers—I speak in the name of monks!—this extremity of our solitude coincides with a beginning of true Christian experience. It is here that the monk is initiated little by little into conversion. The first summit he is called to climb is not that of contemplation but of self-abasement, of humility, and the ideal monk for Saint Benedict, at the summit of his famous ladder, is the publican of the gospel who implores pardon unceasingly.

There, in his solitude and within his own heart, the monk becomes a brother to his fellow men and women and to poor, sinful humanity. There he bears the sin of the universe, not yet as the Good Samaritan who nurses its wounds, nor as the miracle worker who heals it, but as one who is himself sick, leprous among the lepers. If, as an additional boon, the solidarity found there is redemptive, he can hardly dare to believe it since it comes as pure mercy from God on account of Christ who, before him, has borne the same sin.

This solidarity with humanity can go very far, to the point of becoming struggle and agony, the night of senses and of the spirit: a combat of faith that reverberates through the faith of the entire Church. So often, for the contemplative, God seems purely and simply "dead." The monk, in his solitude, is an expert in every human weakness. He is an expert also in atheism. It is by way of his own weakness that he takes the measure of a human being, that he knows what is in a human being. And it is simultaneously by the power of God that he can, for the time being, take the measure of the full stature of the maturity of Christ, who is the uniquely Human in the full sense of the word.

In Community

Unbeknownst to the monk, Christians often perceive only the luminous side of his life. They are struck by his faith, by his disinterest in all vanities, by his prayer that flows as from a spring, and by his humble charity. Above all, monastic communities bear witness. Their common prayer and their loving hospitality attract a multitude.

The majority of monks live this experience of solitude *in community*. The message of fraternity is not alien to Saint Benedict, and this fraternity always refers to the one who, in the midst of his brothers, bears the titles of Christ and holds his place. The monastery is a "church in the desert," a little like that of the Apocalypse, a liturgical community of prayer and adoration as well as a communion of charity where everyone is integrated and abides in stability, where according to Saint Benedict there is a place for the elder who is surrounded with respect as well as for the young person who is affectionately heeded, a community whose capacities for welcome and sharing should never be found wanting, despite its withdrawal from the world.

The insertion of the monastic community in the Churches represents therefore a particular type that eludes sociological categories. Its quality is *spiritual*, pneumatic. Not that it ceases to be concrete in many aspects: just think, for example, of the community at prayer, of the various forms its hospitality takes; the biggest gathering place for young people in France happens to be the monastery of Taizé.

But the quality of this concrete insertion of the monastery derives from a secret depth that flees from visible norms without, for all that, escaping the vague awareness of the Christian people and of so many young seekers. The proximity is even such that it overcomes distances and separations. Saint Thomas said somewhere that the more the solitary hermit is hidden and invisible, the more is he a sign. Thomas thus echoed in his own fashion the famous saying of Evagrius: "The monk is one who is separated from all and united to all."

This spiritual solidarity is not without relevance to a certain number of themes already touched upon. I would like to evoke some of these briefly.

Monks and Priestly Ministry

It goes without saying that the monastic charism springs forth from baptism, but it has nothing to do with hierarchical position in the Church. In itself, the monastic state is a lay state and indifferent with regard to *priestly ministry*. An analogous movement of disinclination toward the priesthood has surfaced over the last fifteen years or so among younger monks. But it is very necessary to discern the real meaning of this. It does not aim at a better insertion in a given milieu. Nor does it express any misgivings with regard hierarchical service, as if it were seen as a "snare." Rather, the disinclination is purely and simply *indifference*, in the best sense of the word, "holy" indifference, if you will, in favor of a greater authenticity and availability for the spiritual adventure that constitutes the stake of the monk's life.

The monk experiences this stake as a veritable "task," a *work* in the strong sense of the word, the sense antiquity gave to it in monastic documents that in Greek call the monk's project simply *to ergon*, "the work." Later, and with more precision, it is called in Latin *opus Dei*, the "work of God" to which the monk devotes himself, body and soul.

I insist on this point because of the misunderstanding that is current in the literature concerning the *aggiornamento* of religious life and that rests, I believe, on a false conception of monasticism. Many orders and congregations have believed—rightly, I think—that they had to break with what has been called a "convent-like" style of life. I do not contest the fact. But the vocabulary employed is a bit unjust in that it risks reducing the monastic project to a structure within which—to push the thought to its logical conclusion—anyone could do just about any sort of work. Of course, there does indeed exist a monastic structure, but it is only a structure, that is to say, unreliable and subject to revision. All its finality is in the work it makes possible. This work is the irruption of the gift of God into the heart of a man or woman and into the fabric of fraternal communion. It addresses itself to the whole person and claims him totally, body and soul, just as it likewise overtakes the group and its whole dynamism. And it lays hold of the concrete person in his crucified flesh, in his fasts and wakeful vigils, in the prayer that will never cease to rise up in his heart, all the way, when the time is ripe, to the light of the transfiguration. The heart of the monk and of the monastic community thus becomes a breach in the opaqueness of the world, through which the light of God infiltrates the universe.

This "work," however, cannot dispense with some *structure*, but a structure that expresses the very rhythm of the search for God. Observances have been criticized, and this was necessary. What no longer expressed anything was allowed to fall away. We undertook the task of purifying and adapting. Above all, we henceforth conceive of observances differently. For us, the monks of today, they are before all else a method of prayer, a technique of recollection, a way to strip down the ego and renounce all desire. In the one who thus abandons himself, the observances open an "empty space" or, better, a depth where God rises to the surface of the human heart.

It is by design that I have just employed vocabulary derived from Zen. This permits me to stress an unexpected solidarity of the monastic tradition with the spiritual quest of numerous believers today. Alongside Yoga, Zen, and other valuable techniques of recollection, the religious tradition of the West itself also offers a proven way to the interior depths of every human being wherein God dwells. The vocabulary may change, the viewpoint may be slightly different. But on the level of spiritual psychology, indeed of anthropology, the methods converge and often even coincide.

An Eschatological Particularity

A final remark concerns the link between the monk and the particular Churches. I have already said that the monastic community is itself recognized as being a particular Church in a certain sense. The monastic "church," of course, does not seek to free itself from the episcopal or sacramental order, but it nevertheless presents itself, within the greater Church, with a very particular project. It even possesses its own structures and hierarchy that have nothing to do with the priesthood. In antiquity, a layman could very easily become abbot. But the particularity of the monastic institute as such is to have exclusive reference to the urgency and the imminence of the kingdom. The monastery is an eschatological reality. It intends to signify what the Churches everywhere await.

By this very fact, the particularity of the monastic Church transcends the particularities and all the provisional oppositions at the heart of the Church, and the monk or the community cedes the right to be identified with any of them. If the monk feels closer to the poor, to sinners, to the meek, and to the peacemakers, it is because the kingdom belongs to them. But this choice should not be understood as exclusive of anyone. To the contrary, it invites and welcomes everyone.

The monastery is also essentially a sort of neutral zone, a zone of free exchange, an ecumenical space offered to all where each one feels at home, whatever one's race, nationality, political affiliation, and social or cultural level—a place where it is already exclaimed in broad daylight that we are all one in Christ. As Saint Benedict already said in terms of the social structures of the sixth century, "slave or free, we all serve the same Lord, we all bear the yoke of the same troop."

This universal face of monastic life must permeate the community itself in its ministry of hospitality. Here lies the test of its authenticity. The temptation of monks has often been to identify with one culture, with this or that class, with certain more or less extremist tendencies. But those who have succumbed to this temptation have paid the price in short order. They have found themselves cut off from the deep movement of the Church and have lost the ear of everyone around them.

This is the way monks envisage their solidarity with the Churches and with humanity. It may seem novel. On reflection, however, you will notice that it is not without points of contact with much of what you experience in your respective charisms.

At the same time, I can say—surely speaking on behalf of all my confreres—that the monk recognizes and feels himself to be in communion with each of the families within the great range of forms of religious life. I would even add that this is necessary if he is to live fully "in his own skin" as a monk.

As for me, if I may be permitted to borrow two extreme examples from this great diversity of forms, I would say: if the hermit were no longer ensconced in the heart of his solitude, and if the Daughter of Charity were no longer immersed in the heart of the multitudes, I would no longer feel at ease as a Cistercian monk. Both the one and the other are necessary to me so that I may be what I would like to be. We are truly in solidarity.

8

Notes from a Pilgrimage

It all began about ten years ago.[1] The event was unexpected and nothing seemed to have led up to it. But its significance could be grasped only with the passage of several months.

We were hosting in our abbey's guesthouse a Romanian Orthodox monk who was little known at that time. Through some anonymous intermediary or connection, he had asked permission to make a retreat in our monastery, which was then as unknown to him as he was to us. His presence was very edifying, we remarked at the time. He had participated in all our offices, all the more easily as he could make out the Latin fluently. He had shared our table. He had even obtained from Father Abbot the special authorization to celebrate from time to time his own Orthodox liturgy. Our abbot had gotten all the necessary authorizations for such celebration, and every precaution was taken so that the unusual situation, rather delicate in those days, might remain as inoffensive as possible.

Our Father Abbot was absent when the visit of the Romanian monk took place. Somewhat timid and excessively prudent by nature, our abbot would scarcely have been eager to grant this monk a larger audience. But, intrigued by the manner of our guest that was on every point so congenial, our Father Prior made use of the opportunity provided by the abbot's absence to invite this Romanian monk to speak to the community assembled in chapter.

[1] This talk was published in 1970.

This was something absolutely new and unheard-of in a Trappist monastery, that is, that a member of a Church not in communion with Rome—hence a *schismatic*—would go up the steps of the throne which at that time dominated the chapter room. At first the monk was going to address us only on one evening but, the subject being far from exhausted at the end of the half hour he had been granted, he was offered another occasion, and he spoke to us on a second evening. In fact, he ended up speaking to us during an entire week. The subject he had chosen—monastic life, or rather, monastic experience—seemed to come straight from his own heart. Right from his very first sentences, something happened. We were suddenly one. There was no longer a *he* and a *we*, Orthodox and Catholics. There were only, on one side and the other, monks who shared the same experience, who recognized each other, in the strong sense of the word, in a grace that was absolutely identical for both sides, a grace that had seized them, that had led them by very similar paths toward a fulfillment and a fullness for which they carried the nostalgia in their hearts: transfiguration in the glory of the beloved, the Lord Jesus Christ.

Nothing and no one could have altered or compromised the intense feeling of communion that had so abruptly imposed itself upon this Latin monastic community: neither the Romanian accent, so tangy, nor the rather literary French spoken by our speaker; neither the inevitable ambiguities (to our ears at least) of a vocabulary very much derived from the *Philokalia*, nor the rigor of the celebrated asceticism that could have evoked fear and discouragement in the hearers. Much to the contrary: in this magnificent proclamation of faith in the monastic charism, we had beyond any doubt been given to each other as brothers.

At the time, it was difficult to analyze the components of this event, difficult too to weigh its importance. We discerned, nonetheless, that something momentous had just transpired, that a spring had just begun to gush forth, somewhere, on a very deep level of the life of the Church, a spring whose force had from the outset impelled us very far down the road to communion and unity, certainly much farther than if we had just travelled the already well-trod paths of ecumenism.

On the day following the first conference, while I was showing my Romanian friend around the monastery, an old monk who met us at a turn of the cloister knelt before our guest to ask his blessing before then embracing him. I learned afterward that he was not the only monk to have made that gesture. A few days earlier, the thing would have been unthinkable, and now it had just happened, very simply, like a flower that opens in place of a bud long swollen and ready to burst. The incomprehension, the prejudices, often so tenacious in the monastic world, had been swept away before the evidence of a lived experience. Called to follow Christ, walking down the same way of obedience, poverty, and consecrated celibacy, the heart and the body straining toward the oblation of unceasing prayer, we had found in each other inseparable and astonishingly close brothers, as all the evidence made plain.

Through this experience, our respective Churches had also come closer together. In what way? We could not have said at the time, but rather we felt it. In any case, a new path toward communion had come to reveal itself, a way that, however, was not entirely new for those who know a bit of monastic history. Perhaps it was necessary to prepare the ground first, to lay down landmarks with prudence and discernment. But it seemed worth the trouble. It was necessary that the path be put to better use and placed at the service of the Church of Jesus Christ, even with a certain urgency.

The event that I have just described was for me the first in a series. On several subsequent occasions it repeated itself in the course of various encounters with monks of the East. The astonishment was always the same. On both sides we felt ourselves forcibly inserted into the mystery of Christ. As the experiences continued to occur, we could better prepare the requisite conditions for them, better understand their importance, better follow and embrace on their basis the ecclesial dynamism. What follows will hopefully help us to take stock of what has been done and to open some perspectives on the future.

Eastern Monks in the West

This is not the place to give even a succinct account of all the ecumenical contacts that have taken place during these past years between monks of our two Churches. Thanks be to God, these meetings tend to multiply in one form or another. We wish here simply to recall the beginnings of a very specific initiative that is now on the way to acquiring permanence in our two Churches.

In March 1968, on the suggestion of an ecumenist friend, I invited Archimandrite Platon of the celebrated Laura of the Trinity and of Saint Sergius at Zagorsk, near Moscow, for a journey to the monasteries of France. He was accompanied by a young hieromonk, Father Serapion. Over the course of two weeks these two beat a path through France beginning from Mont-des-Cats and visiting one by one the Trappist houses, a Charterhouse, some Benedictine monasteries, and a Carmel. On March 21, feast of Saint Benedict, they had the joy of sharing at the Abbey of Solesmes the fervor of the monks there for the patriarch of Western monasticism. The monastic life of the Latin Church was a true discovery for our two Russian pilgrims. Archimandrite Platon himself gave an account of it in an article in the *Journal of the Moscow Patriarchate* that reads like a testimony.[2]

During the summer of that same year, three Greek archimandrites, led by Father Elias Mastroyanopoulos, formerly the superior of the Zoë Movement[3] and now director of the seminary at Tinos, were taking their turn as our guests. They too undertook a similar monastic odyssey through France and, this time, Belgium as well. One of the three, Father Nicholas, has since become Metropolitan of Halkis. Father Elias himself also offered impressions of this pilgrimage in a report that was in part reproduced in *Collectanea*.[4]

These two visits from East to West confirmed on all counts the preceding data of experience. The spiritual bonds established on

---

[2] *Journal of the Moscow Patriarchate* n. 8 (1968): 3–14.

[3] The Zoë Movement, founded in 1907, initiated a remarkable revival of the liturgy and sacramental practice throughout Greece.

[4] *Collectanea Cisterciensia* 31 (1969), supplement to fasc. 3, 11–12.

these occasions, the dialogue concerning the Word received and living in our hearts, the sharing of our experience of monastic life, true *collationes*—"conferences" in the ancient sense of the word— the exchanges of icons, crucifixes, prayer chaplets, and sometimes also relics, expressed more and more clearly a communion that we felt had already been given us in the grace of monastic life.

I remember the emotion shown by our guests when the prior of a Charterhouse came to give them one of the rare typewritten copies of a very imperfect translation of the works of Isaac the Syrian. It was a very rare sort of copy for a Charterhouse and still more rare in the Western world in general at that time, a poor French translation of a dubious English translation of the original Syriac. Nevertheless, a Carthusian had lovingly worked at it in his cell. This interest in the prince of hesychasm and interior prayer in the Byzantine tradition on the part of a Latin monk moved his Greek brothers to tears.

Invited in turn by their three guests, three monks of the West found themselves in Greece and Romania during the summer of 1969. The account given of this trip must be limited by the scope of this article to the most remarkable and intense moments. We will sum up a sojourn of ten days on Mount Athos in Greece; as for Romania, we will furnish a travel narrative of a week among the monasteries of Moldova.

Mount Athos: Ecumenical Reserve

Every Athonite monk is conscious of a call to fidelity to the Tradition, particularly in a Church that today finds herself exposed to influences that are, from his point of view, very poorly defined. Among these influences, one must include the wind of ecumenism that is blowing on Orthodoxy and that more and more penetrates the Church in Greece. The rather general reserve of the monks of Athos vis-à-vis any *rapprochement* with the other Christian Churches is well known. Mount Athos seems little prepared for ecumenism.

On being recognized as a monk or priest of the Roman Church, one must first undergo, according to the general rule, a series of reproaches over usages. These reproaches constituted the indispensable preliminary to every true exchange. In keeping with the culture of the interlocutor, these attacks could concern, for instance, the wearing (or not) of a beard, the cut or color of the habit, the validity of baptism and other Catholic sacraments, the procession of the Holy Spirit, or uncreated grace. Whatever its tenor, this little anti-Roman polemic is generally obligatory. It forms an empirical part of the theological baggage of every good Athonite. For him, no serious conversation with a Latin visitor can be undertaken without staking one's position and excluding any risk of ambiguity. One ought not to take offense but rather try to understand.

Indeed, sometimes ecumenical integrity and rigor of monastic observance go together, and the one seems to be the expression and guarantee of the other. In a certain place it was explained to us, and very courteously, that Catholics could not enter because the monastery was particularly fervent. It must be added that this was the only occasion when we were confronted with such a prohibition on the Holy Mountain.

Moreover, this ecumenical reticence in no way injures the hospitality that is everywhere practiced with an exquisite kindness toward the Orthodox as well as toward the Catholic pilgrim. In the same monastery where access had been officially denied us, at the very moment of our departure, which unhappily coincided with the community's mealtime, an old monk insisted in a most charming way that we stay for lunch.

In another monastery—a sort of small brotherhood consecrated more especially to the Jesus Prayer—the superior first rebuffed us since, not being baptized properly, we had not even received the Holy Spirit. But then he suddenly changed his mind, became lavish in polite attentions, and sat down without difficulty to talk with us about the life of prayer while his brothers served us an improvised meal.

Again there was, in a dependency of the same monastery, a good monk of Cossack origin. By way of prelude to a conversation that was to emerge as one of the most violent accusations against our Church that we heard on Mount Athos, he offered some cucumbers with this delightful commentary: "Take these cucumbers. It's all that I can offer you. But they are full of my love. He who eats them becomes my brother."

A Pastoral Angle on the Pilgrimage

These anti-Roman prejudices of Athos are excusable. The relatively low cultural level of most of the monks must be taken into account. The rather strict break with the world and the inaccessibility of information media also factor in. One must add as well that, even on the level where valuable contacts can be established, in most cases such contacts have been, up to the present, rather disastrous.

In the end, by what means aside from his prejudices can the average Athonite monk know the religious world of the West? Only by what he can perceive and hear of the Westerners who pass through the guest quarters. Now, every type of person can be found among these guests. Relatively few of them are aware of the immense spiritual and ecumenical density that could clothe the activity they are carrying out. Thanks be to God, there are some such people! But the majority of them are hurried tourists who have left spouses or women friends at the threshold of Athos, in a little hotel of Ouranopolis or Ierissos. Their devotions will necessarily be made in haste so that they may not cause their vacation companions to get bored while they wait for their return. Among them there are of course some Christians vaguely interested in spiritual things, often even priests on a vacation circuit who, between Salonika and the Bosphorus, are happy to be able to devote some days to a sojourn on Athos. But very few, despite their doubtless sincere interest, are truly sensitive to the demands of what one could call the "poetry" of a pilgrimage to Athos.

I am thinking of the sort of European tourist that none of us wishes to condemn simply because he walks around in shorts and short sleeves, the shirt generously opened to the rays of the sun. But for goodness' sake! At the most critical moment of a conversation he considers ecumenical, he ought not to reveal his identity and throw in the face of the stupefied monk the last and, as he may suppose, most decisive of his arguments: "But, you know, I too am a priest, a Catholic priest!" He should first of all recall that, while he is there on vacation, he represents the Church only in a relative way and often not at all exhibiting those spiritual values that monks would like to discover in such a person and that, once more, they will be aware of having sought in vain.

On the other hand, there are at Athos relatively numerous erudite pilgrims, sometimes even religious or monks, on a scholarly journey, in search of manuscripts, icons, or frescoes. Perhaps the monk of Mount Athos feels himself more honored by this type of visitor. But if the interest of this researcher is too narrowly focused on the specialty that is his, then his example, above all if he is a cleric or even presents himself as a monk, can only reinforce in the mind of the Athonites that image of a Latin Church entirely profane or too intellectual, without a taste for either asceticism or mysticism.

This reminds me of the example cited by one of these Western scholars, who was scarcely more than that, to prove the low level of human culture that he seemed to have met with among the monasteries of Athos. At the end of his long microfilm sessions in the library of one famous monastery, he bade farewell to the Father Librarian, thanking him for having made his task easier. The latter fixed his large blue eyes on the scholar, bowed his head, and said to him in all simplicity, surely in a tone of humble reproach which, however, escaped the notice of the one he addressed: "Are you sure you haven't wasted your time? Would you not have done better to weep for your sins?" The roar of laughter with which my intellectual friend took his leave, however innocent and full of fraternal frankness it may have been, must have forever confirmed the good Athonite in his conviction that Latin monks belong to a world that is irreconcilable with the one in which he lives and breathes and profoundly foreign to the spiritual reality that he experiences throughout the course of his life.

These examples are invoked to show that a fruitful ecumenical encounter between monks of East and West cannot be improvised. It demands a serious intellectual preparation. But above all, it requires a certain experience of the things of the Spirit, a certain discernment of all that pertains to the charism of the monastic vocation. It is precisely at this level that Athonite monks can be met and understood, as indeed they wish to be.

Let's make no mistake about it: even among the best of these monks, their ecumenical reticence does not derive solely from a lack of information. It may also be the fruit of true spiritual discernment. There are without a doubt some among them who are true *dioratiki,* that is to say, monks "who see through the social persona," or, in our Western language, "who read hearts." They can recognize us for what we are.

Ecumenical Hopes

Mount Athos represents, therefore, one of the most important centers of this ecumenical reticence in the East. In this respect, the spontaneous reaction of the average Athonite differs notably from that which the Latin monk evokes in other monasteries in Greece. In most of them, this reticence has been shed, in the course of these past years, in favor of an attitude of fraternal welcome. The desire to know each other better, to visit each other, to be mutually enriched by contact with the other, has come more and more to predominate.

On Mount Athos itself, there are several places where ecumenical interest flowers. We need, first of all, to make a distinction between the Greek monasteries and those that belong to other ethnicities of the Orthodox world: Russians, Romanians, Bulgarians, or Serbs. The welcome one receives at the Serbian monastery of Khilandari, for example, lingers as an unforgettable memory. Not only were we welcomed with joy, but we also felt as if they had been waiting for us for a long time. Indeed, during a conversation that extended late into the night, almost until the hour of rising for Vigils, one of the monks amicably reproached the Western monks for having taken so long before coming on pilgrimage to Athos.

Within the Greek monasteries themselves, islands of ecumenical openness are surfacing little by little. This is due in part to the vocations of young men who, for one reason or another, have a more direct knowledge of the Latin Church. There are those who were born in the West and have had the opportunity to travel before entering at Mount Athos. Some of them have even drawn very near to our Church. The Father Hegoumen of the young community of Stavronikita, for example, attended the faculty of theology of the University of Strasbourg. One of his confreres likewise studied theology at a Catholic university. We can thus understand how it is that the group of young, dynamic, and fervent university-educated Greeks gathered around them—a group that never ceases to attract vocations—opens easily to the perspective of new contacts with monks of the West.

Our journey to Stavronikita was one of the most blessed moments of our pilgrimage. Rarely does one find a monastic community that is so firmly rooted in the Great Tradition and, at the same time, so peacefully open to the great demands of our time. And this takes place without reducing the purity of the interior search that is pursued faithfully along the lines traced by the great hesychast tradition. "To be present to God is to be present to every epoch at the same time," softly insisted Father Basil, the Hegoumen.

It was to him that we gave, before leaving Stavronokita, the little relic of Saint Benedict that we had been carrying with us on pilgrimage. The gesture was solemn and full of meaning. "We accept this gift with joy. It is of great value," Father Basil responded to me. Henceforth, as a sign of communion in the same spiritual tradition, Saint Benedict will have his place of honor on Mount Athos, among the Fathers of Byzantine monasticism venerated on the Holy Mountain.

Other Athonites, without leaving the East, have been put in contact with Western monasticism indirectly through studies. They are not numerous on Mount Athos. Among them, the beautiful figure of Father Theoclitos stands out as especially remarkable. He is one of the best theologians of monastic life, famous however for a certain intellectual conservatism and for his demanding positions, unfavorable to the Catholic Church. He spends his life in solitude, in a hermitage that faces his monastery and in which he devotes himself principally to the translation of the *Philokalia* into demotic Greek. It is also there that he receives a growing number of pilgrims and spiritual sons. He has the aura of a truly enlightened man—a sort of oracle on the Holy Mountain—and this, despite his relative youth: he is scarcely over forty. His approach is extremely direct; his gaze, piercing; his speech, incisive.

He graced us with two conversations that permitted a surprising feeling of closeness. Our Trappist spirit put him immediately at ease and seemed to have piqued his monastic curiosity. The exchange came back again and again to prayer, to the activity of the Holy Spirit within us, to spiritual direction, and to the uncreated grace that transforms us in Christ. With the *Philokalia* between us, we tried better to formulate the experience and preoccupations of each of our spiritual traditions. Often, the vocabulary of one side or the other had to be defined more clearly. Sometimes summary judgments had to be retracted. Thus, ways opened up by which we might draw ever closer to each other. For, in actual fact, it was with Christ between us two that the conversation pursued its course and we discovered ourselves much more in accord than we had supposed when we first met. That is my conviction and I know that Father Theoclitos, for his part, understood it in the same way.

But, besides ecumenical sympathies that can be still explained in terms of preliminary contacts, there are others that are much less explainable within the habitual climate of Mount Athos and, for that reason, are perhaps more significant. They bloom, often in a most unexpected way, like flowers of secret love, evident signs of the work of the Spirit and indications of a deepening communion.

Generally, it is in the wake of an exchange that, little by little, this sympathy reveals itself. Once the anti-Latin grievances of the interlocutor have been exhausted, it suffices to pose to him abruptly the true problem which, for many of the monks of Athos, is the only problem: "Father, how do you pray?" After the initial moment of astonishment has passed—astonishment that a Latin could actually take an interest in such a subject—the Athonite easily lets himself be drawn into the game, if one can employ such an expression here. In reality, at issue here is a "game" that is extremely serious and grave: it is the game of letting oneself be won over, on one side and the other, by the irresistible climate of such an exchange, which is the climate of the Spirit. In the measure that the conversation is prolonged, that the questions receive responses, that the experience is transparent and truly shared, that one recognizes one's own ideal in that which is at the center of the other's concerns—to that extent spiritual ties are formed. Without yet realizing it, we have mutually introduced each other into the same kingdom, which is that of Christ, into the same interior temple, that of the heart where the Spirit celebrates unceasingly within us. The ecumenical event once again realizes itself. And we leave each other as true brothers, more and more astonished, irritated perhaps, by the theological and ecclesiastical barriers that, of course, still remain and keep us apart.

Sometimes gestures are created spontaneously that aim at expressing this communion, gestures that once would have been unthinkable but that, today, already cross as if naturally the borders that were still in place just yesterday, gestures that escape us to our most total mutual surprise.

I remember precisely a scene that overwhelmed our guide and interpreter, the excellent Dimitris, a young Orthodox theologian of Salonika. At the end of a long exchange, the hegoumen of a monastery invited us to follow him into the Church to venerate the relics. Among them there was, I believe, a relic of a father of the Church. With all the requisite solemnity, the hegoumen exposed the relic. Then he invited us to kiss it. Did I take sufficient account of the great favor he had just shown me? Or did I simply wish to express my gratitude? At all events, the fact is that I proposed to my two companions that we chant the antiphon *O Doctor Optime* in honor of the holy Doctor, and I expressed the same wish to the Father Hegoumen. He became visibly disturbed and lowered his eyes. Then I saw Dimitris who, suddenly, began to blush. I understood then that I had committed a *faux pas*, but it was too late. What to do now? I turned to the hegoumen, wishing to retract my request. It was, however, once again too late.

Now he, with a movement of the head, without ever looking at me, acceded to my wish. And it thus happened that some Latin monks, certainly for the first time in centuries in a church on Mount Athos, intoned one of their antiphons in honor of the saint that they were venerating. Still very moved, Dimitris pointed this out to me as we left the church. But now his face was radiant. The hegoumen, silent and peaceful, was continually looking upon the relics of the great Doctor, but he too must have recognized the fact. It must be added that, after having introduced us into the church, taking every precaution, he locked the door behind us.

"When Monks Come from the West . . . We Will Understand Each Other"

Among still other Athonites, one notices how, even prior to any encounter with Latin monks, they are already predisposed to ecumenical dialogue. At times, they even have a presentiment of the event that occurs.

One thinks, for example, of the venerable hegoumen of Dionysiou, Father Gabriel, who showed us the greatest respect when he learned that we were monks and Trappists. Not for one moment of our visit was he wanting in charity toward us, behaving like a father toward his own children. Besides, his monastery was somewhat famous as the "La Trappe" of Mount Athos, he assured us, on account of its rigorous observance.

Among my memories, the visit to the hermit Paissius has perhaps pride of place. He lives alone in a hermitage that is one hour by foot from Stavronikita, of which he is the spiritual father. Our friends in Athens recommended him to us and, upon our arrival at his monastery, the Father Hegoumen insisted that we not fail to pay him a visit. "Besides," he added mysteriously, "he must be waiting for you." The fact is that, already for the last several months, Father Paissius had expressed to his hegoumen the desire to be put in contact with Latin monks, when the latter should happen to come to Mount Athos: "'When monks come from the West,' he confided to me, 'bring them to me. We will understand each other at once.'"

This saying of Father Paissius made a vivid impression on us. How could we not welcome it as a word of life on the part of someone whose spiritual discernment is recognized by all on the Holy Mountain? It summed up perfectly the intention of our pilgrimage and was, moreover, realized in the course of a two-hour conversation.

There were four of us, seated on very low seats. The hermit himself was crouched on the ground. He responded to or asked questions as he poured us fresh water or cracked open nuts that he insisted on offering us. If someone had told me that we were to meet Saint Isaac the Syrian in person, come back down to earth in our midst, I would not have imagined him otherwise than with the features and charm of Father Paissius: the same sweetness, the same tenderness for us, the same humility, the same clear look of dark and lively eyes, down to the silences that regularly interrupted the conversation like pauses during a liturgical cele-bration that render more dense the words that are progressively born from the silence. The life of Father Paissius is quite simple. Every three hours, he interrupts his work or his rest for an hour of prayer. The latter is divided into an initial quarter hour of *metanias* or prostrations, another quarter hour devoted to the regular office, and the last half hour reserved for the Jesus Prayer. These are, for him, the times of explicit prayer, even though his prayer never really ceases in the broader sense. At work as well as at the time for his reading, within the cell just as when he is outside facing the beautiful panorama that stretches out before him all the way to the sea, Paissius has received the grace to pray unceasingly. While we were approaching his hermitage, hearing nothing more than the impressive silence of Athos, when we had not yet been noticed, we heard his voice in song.

When we parted, he wished at all costs himself to make us a path through the thickets up to the little dusty road that leads to Karyes. Our joy was overflowing. We had found a father and a master. Someone who had received us as his brothers and had expressed to us his joy over our Cistercian *typicon* (rule of life), which we had tried to explain to him; someone who had recog-nized us as children of the same monastic charism and as his own brothers, incomparably younger than he, of course, and who would carry us henceforth in the solitude of his prayer.

The recollection of these few encounters suffices to prove that the ecumenical reticence can be prevailed upon, even on Mount Athos. A dialogue between monks not only shows itself to be possible but has already taken place. Yet again the event came to pass. It is certainly called to repeat itself and to deepen further still in the measure that, on one side and the other, we remain docile to this grace.

Perspectives on the Future

The demands of this docility are many and are not merely on the level of technique. Obviously, only the seriousness of spiritual experience shared fraternally permits this mutual recognition in the Spirit that is the kernel of all monastic ecumenism. In the future, in the midst of analogous experiences, the West will see how to put to the proof the authenticity of its spiritual life. As for the East, what took place in the course of our brief pilgrimage of last year already serves as verification of the quality of the spiritual life lived there by some.

At the same time, this affirmation makes possible a response to the question frequently posed to someone returning from Mount Athos: "Is there still hope for the survival of monasticism on Mount Athos?," and to this other question which the first almost necessarily implies: "Is there still a true spiritual life on Mount Athos?"

It is always difficult to respond to such questions. The difficulty is all the greater in the present case, where the visitor could only meet with those who live at the edge of Athonite monasticism, those charged with maintaining relations with the outside world. The same holds true when, as is often the case, the visitor does not utilize the criteria necessary to support his judgment.

My personal experience of Mount Athos is very restricted. But the little I saw with my own eyes, the few spiritual fathers to whom I could draw near and whose words were for me a source of life—this suffices, I think, for me to dare to express an optimistic appreciation. Through forms that may seem outmoded and undermined by a sterile conservatism, the true tradition shines through even today by means of witnesses who are, in their fashion, true eyewitnesses of the mystery of Christ. At Athos, one can meet those who have seen and those who desire to see. The former and the latter come to abide together in one common quest and participate in the same reality of grace. Is this not the sign that the mystery of the Church is being built up there and that God has fixed his abode in that place? For "where the fathers meet with their sons," said Saint Ammonas, the disciple of Saint Antony, "there God is present on both sides."[5]

This personal testimony is corroborated by that of our guide, the young theologian of Salonika. As an interpreter, he assisted at all our conversations and undoubtedly knew better than we how to register the nuances of the reactions of our Athonite interlocutors. This was not his first visit to Mount Athos. But at the end of our journey, he confessed to me his view that monastic life had evolved considerably. Until the present, he had had difficulty seeing a place for it in the life of the Church. It had appeared to him to be alien to the impact that the Church seeks to have on the modern world. But now it seemed to him that monasticism represented a very great opportunity for the Greek Church as well as for ecumenism among diverse Christian confessions. This spontaneous witness of a young Orthodox theologian overwhelmed me. Can one see in this the proof that dialogue among monks is not only beginning to bear fruit among themselves but is also even destined to cast light on every level of the Church?

Hopes in Romania

Our pilgrimage in Romania was limited to the monastic complex of North Moldavia, more or less grouped around Neamţ. This region was, so to speak, a monastic territory. Even today, this corner of the Carpathians is almost exclusively monastic

---

[5] Ammonas, *Lettres* 6.2, in A. Louf, *Lettres des Pères du Désert*, Spiritualité Orientale 42 (Bégrolles-sur-Mauges: Éditions de Bellefontaine, 1985), 26.

and, in that respect, bears a certain resemblance to Mount Athos. Around Neamţ, in the shaded valleys, on the verdant plains or on the high-wooded summits, in the clearings or under giant evergreens, the sketes—sometimes as large as a village—and the hermitages follow one after another, almost all prospering.

During our travels in Moldavia, the monastery of Sihastria was our home base. The Father Starets (which is how one refers to a monastic superior in Romania) and the little colony of monks that surround him welcomed us with the considerateness of a charity beyond words.

Sihastria was once a hesychastic—that is to say, contemplative and eremitical—dependency of the famous monastery of Secu, five kilometers away. A dozen or so kilometers farther on, there rise up the imposing buildings of Neamţ. These names suffice to remind us that we find ourselves at the heart of that hesychast Moldavia where, toward the end of eighteenth century, under the direction of Paissius Velichkovsky, the *Philokalia* was translated into Slavonic.

Of all the monasteries currently occupied by monks, Sihastria is the most hidden and, in a sense, also perhaps the most prosperous. Quite withdrawn at the base of the valley of the Secu, where the road becomes barely passable, protected from tourists by the absence of any official museum, admirable above all for the fidelity of its residents to the philokalic tradition of recollection and prayer, Sihastria constitutes for the pilgrim, from wherever he may hail, an ideal haven of hospitality and peace.

When it is directed to the Latin monk, this hospitality is truly without reserve. It is openness and charity, without pretense or limit. One feels a bit like a brother long lost to view whose return occasions a joy without the slightest shadow. And if there were any reserve or astonishment, it would be of the order of such a question as: Why did you not come earlier?

As for the separation between the two Churches, it is hardly remembered. There isn't any make-believe going on, but there is little to bring the separation to mind since the joy at having found each other again is so great. Communion is practiced as far as can be reasonably done in our day, through exchanges and liturgical prayer. It stops short, of course, of sharing in the Sacrament, but with a mournful regret. In the liturgies at which we had the joy to assist, at the moment of eucharistic communion, the Father Starets disappeared for a moment behind the iconostasis only to reappear presently, carrying a platter with three pieces of bread and three goblets of wine, all unconsecrated. It is a gesture of communion that the Byzantine liturgy reserves for the bishop when he assists at the Divine Liturgy without taking sacramental communion. Could there be a rite expressing with greater eloquence the desire and the urgency that we all experience at these moments to be still more united to each other?

This openness of Romanian Orthodoxy toward the Latin Church is explained to a large extent by the awareness that the former retains of belonging ethnically and culturally to the Latin world. This awareness is very acute and thrives everywhere. It is the awareness of a national patrimony, indeed, of a national vocation. One can already recognize it in the ease with which most of the monks, little cultured though they be, read and often speak the French language, which immediately increases tenfold the possibility of contacts. But it appears above all in the feeling of their occupying a particular position among the autocephalous Orthodox Churches, a position due to the blending of geniuses and cultures that gave birth to the Romanian people. The Slavic saturation was long and profound, but the Latin stem was never abolished despite the many grafts practiced over the course of history. The national sentiment seems always to have swung between the two complementary poles of Romania's personality, the Latin and the Slavic. This bipolarity confers on it its originality and richness. Perhaps today it also assures it of an exceptional efficacy on the level of dialogue between East and West. For if the Romanian Church is fully Orthodox, it is also fully conscious of representing rather a type of *Latin* Orthodoxy, as a friend there attested, and, on this basis, of being promised an exceptional ecumenical career, if God so wills.

A Purified Monasticism

When it comes to monasticism, this ecumenical ambition is entirely legitimate. The qualities assembled from its theological

reflection and its spiritual experience render Romanian monasticism very apt to enter into fruitful contact with the Latin world.

This quality of spiritual fervor is what strikes above all the
Latin monk who comes to Romania. One may remember how,
at the end of the eighteenth century, Moldavian monasticism
became the cradle of Slavic hesychasm from which, thanks to
channels that go back to Romania, the spiritual movement of
the *starchestvo* (the *startsy* of Optina included) developed progressively in Russia. After the Second World War, a second hesychastic renaissance has had the time to develop in the Romanian
Church on the impulse of a Romanian translation of the *Philokalia*. From this new "Philokalic springtime"[6] there burgeoned a
certain number of spiritual fathers who, to the present day, hold
authority and make new disciples in Romanian monasteries.
Since that springtime, in fact, Romanian monasteries began to
attract a great number of novices. The *sketes* and the hermitages
were repopulated.

Suddenly, the spiritual awakening was put in jeopardy by
the Stalinist persecution that was brusquely unleashed against
monastic life. This persecution became the crucible in which the
new attraction to a life of silence and prayer would be purified.
Some were sent to prisons where they suffered or died. Others
had to return at least temporarily to secular life. Some fortunate
ones took refuge in forests or mountains, and here they rediscovered the most rigorous solitude of primitive monasticism. All
these places and situations became the providential spaces where
Romanian monasticism was purified of its dross and found itself
compelled to retrieve the purity and transparency of its origins.
In all truth, God took at its word the seriousness and generosity
of this monastic renewal.

Its fruits endure even now. Since the beginning of the
de-Stalinization process, the rigor of repression has progressively
relaxed. The monks have reoccupied their monasteries and the
spiritual tradition has been taken up anew. Pilgrims and young

---

[6] A. Scrima, "L'Avènement philocalique dans l'Orthodoxie Roumaine,"
Istina 5 (1968): 295–328, 433–74.

people aspiring to monastic life arrive in great numbers. Often, the civil authorities have facilitated things. Several monasteries have been restored with perfect taste. Monks and nuns live there now as salaried government employees charged with continuing the monastic life and welcoming visitors and tourists. It is not yet possible to foresee what the future holds. But it is permissible to wish that the leaders of the Romanian Church may be sensitive to the possibilities for ecumenical exchanges and contacts that their country's monastic tradition offers the Churches today. Romanian monks occupy a key position at the hinge of Byzantium and Rome, a position so exceptional that it could one day be transformed into an important stage in the *rapprochement* between East and West.

As for symbols of this communion, among so many other memories of dear Moldavia, I will evoke only the evening and the night passed in a secluded hermitage in the heart of the woods right by Sihastria, where I shared in the life and prayer of a young solitary by the name of Martinian, only forty years old. We spoke no common language except for that of prayer and charity. I remember the recollection and infinite gentleness of his face, peacefully framed by two broad cascades of blond curls that covered his shoulders. I thus had the grace to be a guest of his friendship, which was truly royal, although I would probably have preferred to have more free time for prayer. But his charity wanted to load me nonstop with tokens of kindness, and I found myself entirely disarmed before the very moving humility of his gestures. No hour passed without him bringing me some dish he had prepared or some product from his sheepfold. Each time he remained for a long while at my side, without speaking, with only an unending smile on his face and a peace beyond any particular feeling. I gave him an icon as a gift. The next day he brought me a little cross that, during the night, he had carved in ivory according to my specifications. Then, still smiling, he led me back through the woods to the monastery. The day of my departure from Sihastria, very early in the morning, he came down from his hermitage in haste and appeared suddenly beside the car at the very moment when we were about to leave. One last time he had wanted to express his friendship and his total presence in Christ.

A Certain Foretaste

Better than any abstract reflection on monastic life, these few flashbacks from a pilgrimage will enable the reader to understand the meaning and import of the bonds that can be created in this way between monks of diverse Christian confessions. However one approaches these ties, the balance sheet already appears very positive on both sides.

This is obvious for the Latin monk who undergoes this experience in light of the particular needs that he feels today. Threatened by doubt, perhaps even doubt of his vocation, facing numerous challenges in his own Church that call into question anything that smacks of the structures or profound attraction of monasticism, he is consoled by the discovery of a grace entirely identical to his own and lived with a great generosity. It is thus a current of the living tradition that emerges before his eyes, a new ray of the *Orientale lumen*, greeted in the twelfth century by William of Saint-Thierry,[7] for which Western monasticism periodically feels the nostalgia and the need, at the heart of its crises.

But the event is just as important for the Eastern monk and, through him, for the Church that he represents because, for the majority of them, the encounter with a Latin monastery or with Latin monks represents a first contact with the spirituality of the West, thanks to elements that are directly comparable. In this way, they discover another face of the Latin Church, until now considered suspect of activism and secularization. On both sides, suddenly, beyond exclusive jurisdictions, beyond the theological formulas so difficult to harmonize, they *recognize each other* in the same evangelical experience of renunciation, prayer, and a humble life of love in devotion to Christ. In this mutual recognition, prejudices fall away and misunderstandings are cleared up. Of course, as an ecumenist recently remarked, the theological

---

[7] See William of Saint-Thierry, *Golden Epistle* 1.1.

problems persist at their own level, but "this love transforms the data of these problems and produces the premonition that a certain unreality already attends them, without one's seeing exactly how."[8]

Beyond this mutual recognition that can be exteriorly corroborated, one can foresee still more profoundly in these encounters a possibility of more intimate communion, indeed, more *original* communion, since it is situated at the very *sources* of the spiritual life and of the Church. Such communion belongs to the *paradosis* or "handing down" of the monastic charism, a veritable transmission by the Spirit, creating bonds of paternity and filiation.

On one day or another, by this sort of ecumenical predestination that periodically washes over us and which is one of the means by which the Holy Spirit signifies the urgency with which he moves us toward each other, a word of life is solicited and transmitted between monks who are still separated by ecclesiastical barriers. It is an important event, this being reached by the word of a brother from the most intimate center of his vocation, suddenly made present to the designs of God that the word has revealed to us. Every monk is familiar with this experience. It is an experience both of death and of life, in the obedience that divests us of a false personality in order to restore our true spiritual countenance. It is additionally a true birth and it presupposes, or creates, a bond of life between the two partners. It is a wholesale cooperation on the plane of the one Spirit that sets them face to face as father and son. It is, therefore, intercommunion in a very strong sense, at the very wellsprings of life, at the point where the separations between Christian confessions have not penetrated.

This experience is fundamental. It should not be absent from the ecumenical effort that today is spreading so widely in so many areas. In itself, this effort does not require the direct collaboration of monks and contemplatives. Much less would it pertain exclusively to them. Every baptized Christian, in his or her graced being, is invited equally to have this experience of communion in

[8] P.-Y. Émery, "Confusionnisme?," *Verbum Caro* 91 (1969): 67.

the Spirit with other baptized persons. Yet one may suppose that the monks who, at the heart of two different Churches, share the same spiritual tradition and transmit its heritage sometimes even with an identical vocabulary, are particularly well equipped to assume this role. Are they not, by their vocation, "revealers of the Spirit," as it were? Through their mutual communion, the spark of the Spirit should easily fly from one confession to the other.

It will probably take more audacity than it took to intone a Latin antiphon in a church on Mount Athos—and more circumspection and interior attention as well. But so often, beyond our initiatives and our hesitations, the Spirit bowls us over with his unexpected interventions. This happened at the end of a long discussion with one of the great thinkers on the Holy Mountain, a truly spiritual man. He spared me no critique or reproach that a man of his culture could possibly formulate against the Catholic Church without, however, abandoning even for an instant a courtesy that was perfect in every respect. Toward the end of this meeting, the idea came to me to solicit from him a counsel for my personal life. I therefore asked my confreres to withdraw for a moment, and I kept with me only my indispensable interpreter. Then I put my question to the elder in all simplicity, as if I were a novice consulting my Father Master. There was no artifice on my part. The problem posed was entirely concrete and I had, quite obviously, need of a counsel, of a *word* in the ancient sense of the term. My interlocutor did not fail to note the significance of my gesture, for I saw him astonished by my question. He suddenly felt that he was being taken seriously by a Latin monk in his role as spiritual father, as if this were nothing extraordinary, as if we were really living from the same Spirit, as if . . . he hesitated for a long moment. Then I suddenly felt that, with some hesitation, he was leaning toward consent. He, in his turn, took me seriously in my spiritual request and, in so doing, gave me credit and validated, so to speak, this movement of the Holy Spirit within me. A wall of prejudices began to crumble, shaken by the force of the event. Once again, communion had given us to one another, without our having been able to foresee it—both of us captured in the "snare" of an interior movement by which the Spirit led us beyond all we could have hoped for.

I will never forget the word of light that he then conveyed to me, fully aware of the responsibility to which I had just appealed, aware also of the consent that he had thus accorded me—not to me personally, but to the Lord, to the Spirit, and finally to the mystery of the Church in which both of us participated. If *intercommunion* means anything, is it not first of all to be sought on this plane where the life of the Spirit springs up and communicates itself? Or where else could communion be stronger and more vital than in this mystery of spiritual birth where one man elicits life in another within a common and total obedience to the Lord and his Spirit?

The sin of the schism is not that this communion does not exist. It is rather that, despite this communion that has already been given us, we have not yet succeeded at formulating any valuable theological statements in which we recognize each other. Above all, it is that we are not yet at the point of offering the quintessential sign of this communion: sharing in the Body and Blood of Christ. Only sacramental intercommunion will complete and perfectly express the reconciliation of the two Churches.

Of course intercommunion of the heart, of which we have just described several steps, anticipates in a very real way between two individuals, on the plane of the Spirit, the union of the Churches to which they belong. Its tendency is to become ever more explicit, to invade entirely the conscience of the Church. One day, it must be owned and achieved in the plenitude of communion around the Body and Blood of Christ in the Eucharist, so that by this means we will arrive at all the cosmic and eschatological amplitude that intercommunion implies.

"When monks of the West come": these prophetic words of a hermit of Athos resonate like a discreet but pressing call. It has already been heard. In Greece, in Romania, and among us in Western Europe, brothers are preparing a mutual encounter through prayer and study. Next summer will witness diverse pilgrimages both to the East and to the West. In this way monks are rediscovering an old family tradition, which was never entirely lost: the pilgrimage in search of an edifying word or example. From the beginning of monasticism, the celebrated deserts and the most competent spiritual masters have cast their light throughout the whole Church through the flood of pilgrims they attracted. From the outset they constituted the high places that prove themselves essentially ecumenical because they rise above ethnic and cultural barriers.

Lived out as the spiritual path of a poor soul in search of the light, the pilgrimage never seemed contrary to solitude but on condition that the pilgrim continually submitted to a lucid discernment. Today as in the past, the modern penchant for escapism may incline the monk to become some kind of tourist or pious gyrovague. His effort would in such a case be vitiated at its very base, and the temptation veiled by an ecumenical fantasy would soon be frustrated by his Eastern hosts.

Perhaps a day will come when it will no longer be necessary to content ourselves with passing acquaintances and fugitive visits. The need may arise to prolong a journey, to live for a time side by side, without calculations and in all transparency, simply because "it is good for us to be here" (Matt 17:4), because the Lord is revealing himself and transfiguring us and the Spirit is holding us together in unity.

One is reminded of Saint Arsenius,[9] who was the tutor to the Roman Emperor's son, before fleeing to become an anonymous pilgrim in the Egyptian desert. One day one of his former acquaintances, finally finding him in his solitude, was shocked to see him, who had such a splendid mastery of Greek and Latin letters, ask counsel of a simple Egyptian monk. But Arsenius did not retract his gesture. Although he had mastered all profane learning, he avowed his ignorance of the spiritual alphabet of his Egyptian confrere. It was this that justified in his eyes his pilgrimage to faraway Egypt and the fact that he would persevere there to the end.

The one who takes up the pilgrim's staff to pay a visit to brothers does so, in the final analysis, because he counts on their assistance in revealing to him the grace that, until now, has remained too deeply buried within his own heart.

---

[9] See *Sayings*, Arsenius 6.

9

Monks and Ecumenism

The Ambivalence of Monasticism

For those of us who are even a little familiar with history, the rapprochement suggested by the title of this conference—"Monks and Ecumenism"—is far from self-evident. Frequently, at the hour of schisms and heresies, monks have found themselves compromised in the clash —indeed, have even been at the center of it—and monasticism has not always appeared to be a catalyst for unity. On both sides of the walls of separation that have progressively arisen between Churches over the course of the centuries, we can see monks whose zeal, far from bringing the Churches together, has served rather to widen the chasm between them. Such zeal may have been well-intentioned but served to little effect and in fact was closer to fanaticism than to the true fervor of charity.

Even more seriously, the very charism of monasticism has itself at times been directly implicated in certain controversies. The monastic East as well as the monastic West has each had its own respective heresies, conforming to the unique genius of each tradition. For the East, this was the heresy of the Messalians who claimed to do nothing but pray, a heresy that many councils condemned in vain since traces of it would reappear through several centuries. The monastic West knew a heresy of a completely opposite orientation around the same period. Wishing to stress the importance of ascetical effort, the Breton monk Pelagius practically abolished the role of grace in this effort. The powerful and radical intervention of Saint Augustine, little appreciated in monastic circles at the time, did not appease the monks at all, and several generations of monk-theologians would endeavor to make more precise the delicate balance between grace and asceticism, in terms that have perhaps left an echo in the Rule of Saint Benedict two centuries later.

In other circumstances, whole Churches would begin or end by opposing each other on the issue of monastic life as such. Once the chasm was dug between two Churches for completely different reasons, monastic life could not help but be dragged into the schism and, on one side or the other, monks end up no longer being able to understand each other even when speaking of the matters closest to their hearts, like the spiritual experience that—on both sides—they are striving to live.

One of the saddest examples of this was the fourteenth-century controversy between the Graeco-Calabrian monk Barlaam, well-versed in scholastic subtleties, and the disciples of Saint Gregory Palamas. The debate concerned the nature of the light of Tabor that enveloped Jesus at the moment when his continual union with the Father expressed itself perfectly. This is the same light to which, in both East and West, monks desire to turn.

Another equally sad case, closer to home, is found at the very threshold of the Reformation in the person of the monk Luther. Luther despaired of an ascetical effort that did not seem to him open enough to the marvelous possibilities of grace, and he supposed himself to be taking the intuitions of Saint Augustine, his father and teacher, to their necessary conclusion. So Luther came to place in doubt the very credibility, in view of the gospel, of a life founded upon the irreversible commitment of monastic vows.

In the face of the separations among the Churches, it is clear that monastic life does not enjoy any presumption of innocence. It bears its portion of responsibility. Nor can it serve as an infallible antidote or a miraculous remedy, since monastic life is itself also called unceasingly to a way of conversion in the light of the Gospel. It is only by keeping this firmly in mind that it will be possible for us to study several opportunities that monastic life might today afford at the heart of the ecumenical effort among Churches.

From the First Monks to Benedict

In order to carry out this exploration, it will be useful to go back up the slope of history for a moment, even farther back than Saint Benedict, to the origins of monasticism. These are already marked by the ambivalence we mentioned at the start. Among the first monks we can discern at the same time an almost visceral defiance of everything that departs from the true faith and an attitude of humble love, with the door open to the possible miracle of an encounter. The solitary may be renowned for welcoming all those who present themselves at his door and for fraternizing even with the bandits of the region, but the heretic who may happen to arrive at his threshold will find the door closed. Certain monks even refuse to pay a visit to their spiritual father, the great Sisoës, if, in order to reach him, they must go through a region infested by heretics.[1] Abba Agathon, who confesses to being a great sinner, would accept any reproach except that of heterodoxy, since those who do not share the true faith, he explains, are separated from God.[2] And among the counsels that Abba Matoës gives to his disciples, in one single utterance he warns of three dangers: "Be not familiar with any woman, do not make friends with children, and let none of your friends be a heretic."[3]

A more ecumenical nuance, however, reveals itself in the great Poemen, one of oldest and perhaps the most universally respected master in the deserts of Egypt. His exceptional discernment here once again cuts through the rigor of the other Fathers and inaugurates the ecumenical destiny of monks. One day, a group of heretics came to pay him a visit. They begin to slander the conduct of the archbishop of Alexandria: Was he not consecrated against the wishes of the priests of the city? Poemen wisely makes no reply. He avoids the discussion. But he does not break communion. Summoning his disciple, he orders him to set a table for his visitors: "Have them eat," he says, "then send them

[1] *Sayings*, Sisoës 48.
[2] *Sayings*, Agathon 5.
[3] *Sayings*, Matoës 11.

on their way, having first wished them peace." This approach is already full of love and ecumenical hope. It is the first irenic dialogue, at the very dawn of monasticism, drawing inspiration almost from the letter of the gospel.[4]

Several centuries later, during the most intense christological controversies, complementary points of view would harden into theological formulas that were henceforth mutually exclusive and whose partisans excommunicated each other. But just then a similar evangelical gentleness was to appear in the Palestinian desert whose spirituality, as we know, has always remained so close to the Word of God. A brother questions Barsanuphius, the famous recluse of Gaza, to learn what he should say if someone asks him to hurl an anathema against Nestorius. To hurl an anathema at a heretic, replies Barsanuphius, is not the role of a monk, above all if, as is certainly the case for Nestorius and his supporters, the heretics already find themselves under the anathema of the Church: "As for you," responds Barsanuphius, "be not at all hasty to hurl an anathema at anyone, no matter who he may be, for he who knows himself a sinner must weep for his own sins without meddling in other affairs."[5] Astonishing collusion between the monk and the heretic, and one that accords entirely with the gospel besides! A sinner himself, how could the monk arrogate to himself the right to condemn a false believer, since neither of them has any hope apart from the mercy of God?

The same brother insists, however, in addressing his spiritual father: In order to convince the heretic of his error, would it not be right to enter into discussion with him in order to defend the true faith? Once again, Barsanuphius responds, this is not the task of a monk, unless by way of exception: "If you really want to help him, speak within your heart to God, who knows what is hidden and who can do even more than you ask of him."[6] One sees here the first trace of a prayer for the unity of the Churches, engraved

---

[4] *Sayings*, Poemen 78.

[5] Barsanuphe et Jean de Gaza, *Correspondance* (Sablé-sur-Sarthe: Éditions de Solesmes, 1972), 699.

[6] Barsanuphe, *Correspondance*, 695.

in the heart of someone who has left everything to follow his Lord even to the heart of the desert, a desert that somehow coincides mysteriously with the heart of the Church.

We do not intend here to pursue this enquiry through the whole course of monastic history. But since this conference seeks to honor specifically the fifteenth centenary of the birth of Saint Benedict, we will pause a moment at his Rule which, as you well know, very quickly became the sole monastic Rule in the West. This Rule already constitutes in itself an ecumenical gesture of exceptional importance since it gives a face to Western monasticism that is in no way dissimilar to that of the East.

One should recall that Saint Benedict is not the creator of monastic life. The latter existed before him and had been transmitted for several generations, from spiritual father to spiritual son. When for the first time Christians, in the name of the Gospel, separated themselves from the community of believers to withdraw into the desert and live a solitary life, cut off from the sacraments, the ecclesiastical world surely did not immediately understand them. It would require some great bishops making good use of speech and pen to attest that such a way of life, however unusual it might seem, was nonetheless inspired by the Spirit of God and could exist in full harmony with the Church. Saint Athanasius, among others, would do this on behalf of Saint Antony in fourth-century Egypt.

A tradition came to be born. Benedict, after so many others, welcomed it in his turn in order to transmit it to those who would follow after him. Therefore, he did not have to become what today we would call the founder of an Order, and such was certainly not his intention. What he wanted most was to adapt to the particular conditions of his contemporaries the body of monastic doctrine and usages that he had inherited from his spiritual fathers. This heritage was not anyone's property. It was a good held in common by the whole Church. Its light had at first shined with particular brightness in the East. Having arrived in the West, it would not take on a different visage. The common age-old traits deriving from the origins of monasticism would always predominate over the legitimate adaptations.

The concern to keep the monasticism of the West close to its Eastern sources was, long before Saint Benedict, the preoccupation of Saint John Cassian, to whom Benedict loves to refer. That concern truly haunted Cassian. Anxious at the signs of decadence presented to his eyes by the monasticism of Mediterranean Gaul in the fifth century, Cassian undertook a long journey, a veritable pilgrimage, to the monastic wellsprings in Egypt and the Holy Land. Later, writing his *Instituta* and his *Collationes* (or "Conferences"), Cassian wished to remind the young abbots of Gaul of the grace common to all monastic life and how it must inspire the reform that he meant to promote among them.

In fact, this monastic grace expresses itself in a body of doctrine and usages that would go back, as Cassian rather rashly supposes, to the apostolic age. This body Cassian qualifies with the astonishing and marvelous name *Regula catholica*, the "Catholic Rule," in the ancient sense of *catholic*, that is to say universal and truly ecumenical. One may recall the meaning lent to this word by Saint Cyprian when he said of the Church that she is at the same time one and universal: *Ecclesia quae, catholica, una est.* Thus we would venture to say that, in the image of the Church, monastic life is one, that is to say always the same, inspired by the same Spirit, oriented to the same search. In this way it is also universal and, in all the Churches, in whatever form it may adopt, it is perfectly recognizable, at once a criterion of unity between the Churches and a sign, among others, of this rich variety that, beginning with the complementary diversity of peoples, weaves the multicolor tunic of the Bride of Christ.

Saint Benedict also positions himself without hesitation at the heart of this tradition, at the same time one and universal. Not only does he make explicit appeal to Saint John Cassian and to the *apophthegmata* of the fathers, but on two occasions, and in rather solemn fashion, he explicitly refers his monks to those whom he hails as *Patres catholici et orthodoxi*, the "orthodox and catholic fathers." In his day, these two adjectives were in no way opposed but designated, as we know, two correlative criteria that must be verified in every theologian and spiritual person: orthodox, that is sharing the true faith; catholic, that is recognized as such by all the Churches.

It will suffice to cite the conclusion of the Rule of Saint Benedict in order to see how, having completed what he modestly calls "this little Rule for beginners," Benedict effaces himself before the Great Tradition that he presents to his disciples. He writes: "For those who are hastening to the perfection of the religious life, there are the teachings of the Holy Fathers, the observance of which leads one to the heights of perfection."[7] *Doctrinae sanctorum patrum*. Who are these Holy Fathers?

Saint Benedict specifies their identity. They are of three kinds. These Holy Fathers are, first of all, the Word of God itself along with all those whom it chooses as ministers: "For what page," continues Saint Benedict, "what passage in the Old and New Testaments, having God for its author, is not the surest norm for the conduct of human life?"[8]

Next, the Holy Fathers are those who are eminent for the holiness of their teaching. Again, I cite Saint Benedict: "What book of the Holy Catholic Fathers does not teach us how to run along the straight path to our Creator?"[9]

Finally, the Holy Fathers constitute a more restricted foundation, since we are dealing here with monastic life, in which context the term signifies the fathers of the monastic tradition, uninterrupted from the origins of the Church. Let us hear Saint Benedict once again: "And besides the *Conferences* of the Fathers and their *Institutes* [he refers here to Cassian] and their *Lives* [that is, the *Vitae Patrum* or the *apophthegmata*], there are the Rules of our Holy Father Basil [witness here the East enthroned in the West] that are nothing else but instruments for growth in the virtues for disciplined and obedient monks."[10]

By way of an addendum, Saint Benedict makes the following confession, so perfectly characteristic of him: "But for us who are lazy, undisciplined, and negligent, they cause us to blush for shame."[11] This glorious Tradition is not the property of Benedict.

[7] RB 73.2.
[8] RB 73.3.
[9] RB 73.4.
[10] RB 73.5-6.
[11] RB 73.7.

It surpasses him on every side. Positioning himself at its heart, Benedict humbly recognizes himself as heir to a grace that burns his lips. In order to transmit it to others, he relies more on the power of God than on his own weakness or that of the brothers whom he addresses.

A Natural Ferment of Unity between the Churches

It does not appear, as noted above, that Saint Benedict ever had any personal involvement in a schism between Churches. His monasticism is peaceably ecumenical. While the Churches were united—even if they came legitimately to differ on more than one point over the course of centuries—the catholicity of monastic life equipped it to be a natural ferment of unity among the Churches. By means of this life, believers of different Churches recognized each other in the identity of the very same grace. Monastic life can thus take on an exceptional ecumenical character. In a certain sense, which bears further precision, it is in a particular way the task of monks, existing at the heart of the People of God, to testify to the unity of all the Churches.

Alas, too often, as we have seen, monks have taken up the contrary role of denouncing this unity. What happens then? Once the Churches were effectively separated, monks were fatally dragged into the schism and aligned with the Church to which they belonged at the time the rupture took place. In certain cases, they could go so far as to identify with the schism and become its most fanatical defenders. In spite of everything, however, and wherever he may be, the monk remains marked by the sign of unity and ecumenicity. He has received a certain experience of God and a taste of God that go far beyond the formulas that try to circumscribe them. He also possesses, through prayer, a sense of the universal communion in Christ that exceeds the visible borders of the Churches such as they have become fixed after the wounds of the great schisms. He feels in a confused way that he must live within a certain ill-defined ecclesiological space, at a point where the partitions erected by the separation have not prevailed and where already those walls are yielding which, as

Metropolitan Platon of Kiev said one day, certainly do not rise all the way to heaven.

Even when he is compelled to recognize the inevitable ecumenical slowness of the Churches, the monk, by the grace he has received, carries within himself a piercing cry for the total unity of all those who follow the same Lord. He bears this unity somewhere within himself. It is given to him in what Thomas Merton has called the "virginal point" that exists in every human being. The invisible, thus circumscribed in his own heart, allows him to experience a plenitude that the exterior schisms have not destroyed, an inviolate point of the undivided Church. If we could all discover it together but for an instant, it would become infinitely easier from this point to welcome the gift of visible unity that the Lord is always ready to bestow upon his Church.

The Monk and His Fellow Christians of East and West

Is it now possible to say more concretely what role monks have to play in ecumenism? If the Catholic monk turns first of all to his brothers of the East, the matter seems relatively obvious. At the end of the nineteenth century, Pope Leo XIII grasped the importance that lay in the preparation of Benedictine monasticism for an encounter with Eastern monasticism. As the Reverend Roger Greenacre has recently noted, this seems indeed to have been one of the principal objectives pursued in the creation of the College of Sant'Anselmo at Rome: to form Western monks who could approach the Churches of the East with sympathy and understanding. True, this papal idea received few echoes at the time. It would be taken up, more than a quarter century later, by the apostolic letter *Equidem verba*, which Pius XI addressed to the Abbot Primate of the Benedictines on March 21, 1924, the Feast of Saint Benedict, in order once again to encourage Latin monks to prepare, even in the name of their vocation, for a more emphatic ecumenical apostolate. The pope insisted at length on the natural bonds that exist between the two monastic traditions. The monastic order as such saw the light of day in the East. Saint Benedict, furthermore, hailed as father of monks in the West, is still venerated as such by the Eastern Churches; the marvelous development of Western monasticism during the High Middle Ages had taken place before the two Churches were separated by the schism. The Benedictine Order, according to the pope, has preserved to this day the traditions of the Holy Fathers and their zeal for the Sacred Liturgy and for the fundamental elements of ancient monasticism.

In the days of Pius XI, however, with the necessarily unionist mentality that characterized nascent Catholic ecumenism, the appeal made to monastic families of the West could not help but carry nuances almost of a crusade. Monastic life thus risked being reduced to an instrument of unionist tactics, perhaps merely more effective than the others. This strategy expressed the hope that, impressed by the monastic fervor of the Church of Rome, the Oriental Churches would be less hesitant to reunite with her.

In actual fact, since the publication of the apostolic letter of Pius XI, monks have never played the role envisioned in such a perspective. Dom Lambert Beauduin, the discrete man behind the inspiration of the pontifical document, was himself to realize partially the plan of Pius XI. He remained watchful in his opposition of unionist tactics. The misunderstanding that resulted between Beauduin and certain Roman circles loomed large in the disgrace that was to haunt him for twenty long years. Yet the stakes were high and the question then posed coincides with our own: What is the ecumenical pertinence of monasticism? Could one make use of it to facilitate the return of one Church to another, as the West might have wished for the East, or the East for the West? Or, on the contrary, will it be necessary, beginning from a communion experienced together as profoundly as possible, to seek to open an entirely new path of encounter and exchange?

Before responding to this question, let us now turn for a few moments to the Churches issuing from the Reformation. Collusion between these Churches and the old monasticism does not immediately rise into view. That is already an understatement and I suppose that more than one reader may find even the mere mention of this possibility paradoxical. Nevertheless, although born of Luther's very negative personal experience of monastic life, the Reformation never ceased to question itself on this subject. Oftentimes Protestant theologians, even recently, have had a presentiment of a certain question that monastic life poses to the Reformation, along with the cherished hope that, on their side also, monks may feel themselves confronted by certain questions that the Reformation poses to them.

Permit me to cite here an appreciation voiced by the famous Methodist historian, Gordon Rupp:

> The Protestant Reformation has contributed notably to the constitution of Europe, and it is generally accepted that this action has entailed a surrender of what one might call the Benedictine spirit. Let us concede as much. Nevertheless, notwithstanding harsh and draconian critiques of monasticism, the priorities established by Luther—God, conscience, and the communion of saints—were also those of Saint Benedict. Martin Luther went to the Diet of Worms impelled by the same motive that led Benedict to Subiaco: he was bound in conscience by the Word of God. With God's help he stood fast, for he could not do otherwise. And the emblem of the Protestant Reformation has always remained a monk struggling in prayer, hunched over his Bible, his unconscious teeming with the images and the words of Scripture, above all those of the Psalter.[12]

This emblem, which Rupp reclaims for the Reformation, could equally be that of monastic life consecrated to the Word of God in *lectio*, praise, and prayer. On both sides, there is equally a question of being seized by a need for conversion and reform. There is, besides, no concept that sums up more fittingly the unfolding of monastic history than *reform*. This history has been a long succession of reforms, each of them attempting to situate the monastic experience fully in the light of the Word of God. It is from reform to reform, from *aggiornamento* to *aggiornamento*, that monastic life seeks to manifest little by little all the riches of

---

[12] Rupp's conference was given at a symposium entitled "A Vision of Europe" in Coventry Cathedral in 1967 and sketches the background, achievements, and significance of Saint Benedict. It was later published in Rupp's book *Just Men* (London: Epworth Press, 1977).

grace that the Lord, through this life, has entrusted to his Church. In order to remain faithful to itself, monastic life has need of reform; it is a constitutive law of its dynamism. In every age it needs a reform to keep it on the straight path of the Gospel. Here the question arises: Could Luther have become the reformer that monastic life was awaiting in his day? His was a different path, and yet it remains near. In a penetrating analysis of the frightful interior combat that brought Luther to renounce monastic life, Dietrich Bonhoeffer has written:

> It was in the failure of the ultimate possibility of leading a pious life that Luther seized upon grace. He experienced, in the bankruptcy of the monastic world, the saving hand of God held out in Jesus Christ. He grasped it in the assurance that all our efforts are vain, even those of the best life.[13]

To this I would venture to add a question: Is the experience of the monk so different from that of Luther, except perhaps that the saving hand of grace touches him and raises him up from within his vocation?

There is in this description of Luther's experience, furthermore, a fundamental element of the monk's experience. A certain image of monastic life, which makes a quasi-pagan appeal to the monk's natural generosity, here suddenly melts away. As in Luther's case, there arrives a moment when the monk is no longer able to rely on his own strength, radically inadequate as it is, for the maintenance of his monastic intent. He finds himself reduced to a weakness that, if joyfully accepted, gives birth little by little to true humility. He is at the mercy of God's mercy, which comes to meet him at that point of poverty where all his natural energies are exhausted. The saving hand of grace can henceforth act freely, and monastic life, if it is indeed possible for a believer, becomes now the only thing it can truly be: a miracle of the Word and of Grace in a believer reduced to his distress and yet "trusting to the point of folly in the mercy of God." Note that this quotation is not from Luther but from Saint Thérèse of the Child Jesus! Saint

---

[13] D. Bonhoeffer, *The Cost of Discipleship* (New York: Macmillan, 1966), 51.

Benedict recognized in the image of the publican of the gospel the icon of the mature monk who, aware of his own sin, no longer dares to raise his eyes to heaven but repeats unceasingly in his heart: "Lord, have mercy on me, a sinner." It is a marvel of repentance, of gentleness, and of true love, humble and universal.

The Reformation never ceased to recall this absolute priority of grace without, for all that, ever arriving—until recently—at a resurgence of monastic life. It may be asked, however, if the evangelical grace of the Reformation does not constitute a particular variant of monastic grace itself, under a very stripped-down and entirely interior form. In addition, the periodic revivals within Protestantism have drawn very near to the borders of monastic life, and some have been able to see in them abortive monastic movements. Did not John Wesley himself confess that, had he not been the founder of the Methodist movement, he could not have finished his days other than as the abbot of a Benedictine monastery? Writes Karl Barth:

> One can cultivate and express many serious objections against the theory and practice of monasticism, old and new, Eastern and Western; but these objections do not touch the will and the intention that stand behind it all. . . . Simply because, first of all, [the monks] seem also to have known at least something of what we thought we thought we knew better than they! But, in addition, because they know something else that ought to give us food for thought.[14]

Monastic life and Reformation are undoubtedly closer to one another in their fundamental intuitions than they at first appear; in any case, they seem to need each other. That is the conclusion drawn, already some ten years ago, by a theologian of the Church of England, Canon Donald Allchin:

> It is only when the doctrine of justification by faith is placed—not to destroy it but to liberate it—within the great current of the Catholic tradition of sacramental or monastic life that this

---

[14] Karl Barth, *Church Dogmatics*, vol. 4, t. 2, 64 (New York: T. & T. Clark, 2009), 9–10.

tradition can freely blossom as an expression of the Gospel. But, on the other hand, it is only when this doctrine is itself placed within the context of which it forms a part, and freed of destructive elements that it contains in the formulation given to it by the Reformation, that it will once again be truly understood and lived as an authentic expression of the Gospel.[15]

A reflection such as this opens a broad perspective of exchange and communion between the grace of monastic life and that of the Protestant Reformation. How can we not place our hope in this Word that both sides are called to utter to each other today and that, if it be well received, will draw our confessions considerably closer together?

Intercommunion of the Heart

I have just pronounced two key words: exchange and communion. They characterize the precise form under which monks, without usually being aware of it, find themselves implicated in the ecumenical process. Very different is the task of the theologian who submits to his critique the theological formulas used in the exchange from the task of the Church authority that discerns the signs anticipating a union whose hour draws near; and different still is the task of monks who, living at "ground level" in the heart of the Church and committed to a total docility to the Word of God and to his Spirit, are sometimes well-positioned to recognize those whom the Spirit has provisionally led along parallel paths but who are already finding their way toward one other.

There is a place here for a truly spiritual, "pneumatic" intercommunion between brothers still separated by the structures of the Churches to which they belong but in whose midst the spark of the Spirit may suddenly fly. Permit me here to recount a personal experience that happened some dozen years ago.[16] The

---

[15] D. Allchin, "La tradition monastique et la Réforme. Réflexions inspirées de Thomas Merton," *Collectanea Cisterciensia* 32 (1970): 73.

[16] See A. Louf, "Notes from a Pilgrimage," chap. 8 of the present volume, pp. 100–111.

incident took place during a pilgrimage to Mount Athos that I
had the opportunity to undertake. This was at the end of a long
discussion with one of the greatest thinkers on the Holy Mountain, a truly spiritual man. He had not spared me any critique or
reproach among those that a man of his culture could formulate
against the Catholic Church. Toward the end of the meeting, the
idea came to me to solicit from him a counsel for my personal
life. I therefore asked those who accompanied me to withdraw for
a moment, keeping with me only my indispensable interpreter.
Then I put my question to him very simply as I would have asked
it of my Father Master when I was a novice. Nor was there any
ruse on my part. The problem posed was quite specific and I
really did need some counsel, a "word" in the ancient sense of
the term. My interlocutor did not miss the significance of my
gesture, and I saw he was bowled over by my question. He suddenly felt himself being taken seriously by a Latin monk in his
role as spiritual father, as if it were an entirely natural thing, as if
we truly lived from the same Spirit. He hesitated a long moment,
then suddenly I felt him leaning toward consent. In his turn, he
was taking me seriously in my spiritual request and, in doing so,
he did me credit, as if it were validating this movement of the
Spirit in me. A wall of prejudices came crashing down, shaken by
the force of the event. Once again, communion had been given
to us both without our having been able to predict it, both of us
captured in the "snare" of an entirely interior situation where the
Spirit was leading us beyond all that we could have hoped for.

I will never forget the word of light that he transmitted to
me then, fully conscious of the responsibility to which I had
just made appeal, conscious also of the consent that he had thus
given me—not to me personally, but to the Lord, to the Spirit, and
finally to the mystery of the Church in which the two of us both
participated. If intercommunion means anything, is it not first of
all at this level where the life of the Spirit rises up and diffuses
itself? Besides, where could communion be stronger, more vital,
than in this mystery of spiritual fatherhood where life is stirred
up in one man by another in a common and total obedience to
the Lord and to his Spirit?

That such an experience of communion should be possible brings home a fundamental reality to which we have already alluded: the persistence, beyond or underneath visible separations on the surface, of a single Church still really undivided and doubtless never separated. One Lord, one body, one baptism, one sole Spirit: all of us believe that this mystery of unity is not absent from us today, and that our Churches, in spite of appearances, all participate in it in a certain way. Nor is it difficult for us to discern concrete places where this mystery sometimes reveals itself transparently. Beyond any doubt, wherever one looks, holiness constitutes one of the privileged places where ecumenism shines forth incomparably. To take up the words of Metropolitan Eulogius: "Men like Saint Seraphim of Sarov, Saint Francis of Assisi, and many others have accomplished in their lives the union of the Churches."

The monastic institution and life according to the Gospel can become another place where the undivided Church makes itself visible. Communion in docility to the same Spirit cannot fail. Such an experience is of capital importance. Beginning from there, ways will emerge whereby one may approach the more delicate domains of controversy, where the theological oppositions will appear henceforth less irreducible and can lead to a deepening of the grace proper to each. The West is called to recover its East, and the East, its West. The two together are continually challenged in this direction by the ferment of the Reformation with its strong evangelical accent. Such a path, taking its point of departure from a certain experience of the undivided Church, may seem the opposite of what official ecumenism tends to assume, that is, addressing frontally the divergent points in the hope of progressively reducing them in order to regain communion. The path of spiritual ecumenism has the privilege of beginning with a communion that is, so to speak, antecedent, already distinctly felt but whose consequences must still be explored. In setting out from such an experience, the ecumenist possesses from the outset a criterion of discernment that will permit him to go forward, boldly but in perfect fidelity to the Holy Spirit. It has never been obvious that ecumenical dialogue must progress first of all by way of successive rational clarifications that gradually become more convincing. Experience suggests the contrary. This dialogue follows life closely and proceeds from it. It advances rather by successive shifts of terrain that are, I venture to say, unforeseeable and irresistible, and that result in a sudden modification of the theological or ecclesiological landscape and thereby cause to appear new configurations of the territory that no one had dared to predict. These shifts in the terrain on the surface of the ecclesial crust are provoked, no doubt, by a new subterranean equilibrium, that is to say, always by an increase in holiness and in love.

When the course of ecumenism thus surges from within, it more easily takes on the qualities of what we have called an inexorable advance toward unity, leaps forward of which recent history has left us illustrious examples among the highest officials of our Churches. And why not? For those really directed by the Spirit of God, there are gestures that escape them to the most complete mutual surprise. The very least this accomplishes is to assure us that it is indeed God in person who builds up and reunites his Church.

This is how monks remain open and docile to the ecumenical grace at work in the Churches. Their contribution is not spectacular. But they seek to hold fast to the sources of the Church, that is to say, to what is deepest in their own hearts. One of the twentieth century's most famous monks, Thomas Merton, marvelously intuited this mystery and undoubtedly experienced it in the secret of his solitude. I now bring this to a close by quoting him:

> If I can unite in myself the thought and the devotion of Eastern and Western Christendom, the Greek and the Latin Fathers, the Russians with the Spanish mystics, I can prepare in myself the reunion of divided Christians. From that secret and unspoken unity in myself can eventually come a visible and manifest unity of all Christians. If we want to bring together what is divided, we cannot do so by imposing one division upon the other or absorbing one division into the other. But if we do this, the union is not Christian. It is political, and doomed to further conflict. We must contain all divided worlds in ourselves and transcend them in Christ.[17]

---

[17] Thomas Merton, *Conjectures of a Guilty Bystander* (New York: Image Books, 1968), 21.

10

In the School of the Psalms

Christian prayer is not born first of all out of the need that humanity feels to express itself to God. It derives rather from the fact that God once addressed himself to humanity. This Word of God to the human race determines all prayer. God takes the initiative. The human role is to remain attentive and to welcome this initiative with joy and thanksgiving.

Now, as Scripture attests, God "spoke to human beings in many and diverse ways" (Heb 1:1). But he did not content himself with pronouncing and inspiring the words that he wanted to speak to human beings. He himself formulated the words that he wanted to hear from their side when they responded to his call. This is the significance of the presence of the prayer of the Psalms in the biblical canon.

At first glance, this may be surprising. Is not prayer essentially the word that the human being addresses to God? But this prayer, by the very fact that it belongs to the Scriptures, seems to have been recognized principally as a Word of God, a Word that he himself has placed in the heart and on the lips of humanity.

Christians and Jews thus have at their disposal a school and a method of prayer that come to them directly from the Spirit of God, since this school and method of prayer have been incorporated into the Word written by God and, for this reason, are inspired by his Spirit. What a privilege and unique good fortune! Is there any other people to whom the Lord comes so close as this: that he should wish to grant us the very words of our prayer?

But in what way is God the author of the Psalter? And how has it come to be that this prayer, originally Jewish, should become also the prayer of the Church and of every Christian who lends it his voice? And how can every believer, in turn, enter into this prayer so as to appropriate it for himself? These questions concern us particularly at this present time when people often ask about prayer and the techniques that lead to it.

Birth of the Psalms

I must repeat that it is first of all God who addresses a word to humanity. Without this action on God's part, which holds indisputable primacy, prayer would never have come to be. God takes the initiative. His Word strikes the heart of the human person, by which I do not first of all mean the Word such as it has been put in writing in the Holy Scriptures, but God's Word above all as absolute event: his all-powerful and completely efficacious intervention in salvation history, in the history of the Churches, and of each individual destiny. Even those who live outside any word of the Bible are reached one way or another by the power of God's Word.

Left to itself, however, the human heart lacks the means of making itself permeable to the Word. It can do nothing but present to it the wall of its blindness, a total absence of sensitivity to the sound of God's voice. Besides, at the first moment of its sounding, the Word of God is often deafening. It seems to make one deaf or blind, simply because it cannot help but reveal the congenital deafness of the one to whom it is addressed.

But things don't stop there! The Word of God is always creative and supremely effective. It bears the power necessary to vanquish all the resistance in the heart. Out of it shines the light thanks to which humanity is able to grasp it. It is not, therefore, content simply to strike the heart—it also opens a wound. It brings back the heart of the one whom it calls and renders it vulnerable: "The Word of God is living and effective, sharper than any two-edged sword, penetrating to the division of soul and spirit" (Heb 4:12).

Thus, every person is liable to be one day handed over to the all-powerful Word. Even without our knowing it, we are continually exposed to this Word. But in what way?

The Word of God wounds us only that we may advance progressively toward conversion and a true "re-creation." It penetrates our weakness to fill us with its strength. It first proclaims our sin that it might then shower us with forgiveness and mercy. It does still more: it makes its dwelling within us.

The Word of God seizes our heart so as to enable it to seize the Word in its turn. It comes to abide in the heart in order that the heart may at length abide in the Word. Little by little, the heart makes of it its exclusive nourishment. It unceasingly ruminates on it, assimilates it, and is transformed by it. The heart comes to need a long and patient listening to the Word of God, whose flavor penetrates us bit by bit, whose power, gentle yet irresistible, draws us and sustains us unawares within its field of energy. Heart and reason emerge from it purified. All the desires unite to espouse the desire for God, whose Word diffuses a contagious joy. In this way the Word of God, frequented over a long time, truly re-creates the one who applies himself to listen to it. And suddenly a new outpouring is already about to occur.

From this slow assimilation, from this interpenetration between the human heart and the Word, one day the Psalms were born. They were born from a heart that, by dint of having listened and made itself permeable to the Word, had become so identified with the Word as to become itself the Word. The Psalms were born of a heart fertilized by the Word, that irresistibly gave birth in its turn to a new Word, a Word that is at once its own and God's: "My heart has brought forth an excellent word" (Ps 44:1).

The Psalms are at the same time the fruit of the human heart and of the Spirit of God. They are the fruit of the human heart because they reflect the experience a person has come to know within his heart. And they are the fruit of the Spirit inasmuch as this experience has been opened up and unceasingly directed by the Word of God itself. It was the same Word of God, inspired by the same Spirit of God, that brought forth a new fruit through the heart of a believer. The Psalms are a human prayer, born from the Word of God, but at length they become the Word itself. This Word of God returns to God, but not without having borne its most exquisite fruit: the prayer of a human heart.

This is a vivifying process of which the most striking example is surely left us in her *Magnificat* by Mary, the praying woman at the heart of the Jewish people and on the threshold of the Church. This marvelous song both does and does not belong to her. It is indeed the fruit of her heart, just as Jesus is the fruit of her womb. But it is still more the fruit of the Word, just as Jesus is the only-begotten Son of the Father. All the words of her song came to her through her tireless rumination on the Scriptures. Her song, however, is not for all that a banal plagiarism. Quite the contrary, it is entirely informed by the unheard-of experience of Mary, who has just conceived by the Holy Spirit. It has gushed forth from a heart filled with the Holy Spirit and pregnant with the hope of all peoples. It is authentic prayer, stirred up by the Word of God and expressing the mystery that Mary is now living. At the same time, such a prayer is also the prayer of the Church. Continuing the impetus of the Virgin, the whole Church will forever be able to recognize itself in the *Magnificat*. Alongside the other Psalms of the Bible, the song of the Virgin was to become the great prayer of thanksgiving and praise for all those who have been saved.

Poetry that Prays

The Word of God that resounds in the Psalms does not in every respect resemble the Word of God such as we find it elsewhere in the Bible. The psalmists would say that it has become song, jubilation, dance, the clapping of hands. It adopts a certain rhythm and often demands some instrumental accompaniment. We might say that, in the Psalms, the Word of God has become poetry.

It is not without significance that Christian prayer took its origin from poetic words. We have just referred to the manner in which God's Word wounds the human heart so as to give rise to prayer within it, and this already orients us toward an experience of the poetic type. The Word of God does not address itself only to the conscious intelligence; rather, it takes hold of human intelligence in its totality, encompassing all the depths of the unconscious in the widest sense of the term. It does not merely communicate to us a truth but rather sets us before absolute Beauty. A Word so near to the splendor of God, so full of the Spirit, could not help but have recourse to poetry. So must also prayer do the same.

All human speech is borne by a mystery. Born of the heart and breath of a human being, it conveys a certain human experience it is capable of transmitting to others. It can resonate on many different levels. If human speech becomes poetry, then it deploys its potentialities to the maximum.

In everyday speech, and still more in the precise vocabulary of scientists and philosophers, the evocative power of the word is reduced to univocity, only one level of meaning, and this reduction is indispensable for the clarity of the exchange; but it remains inevitably on the surface of human existence. Poetry, on the other hand, like love, restores to the word all its harmonies. The poetic word invades the person who hears it on all the levels of his being. It is no longer merely a concept but also light, warmth, music, color, intoxication, nostalgia, an undefined sense of the humility of things and beings and of the infinite reality that they strain to touch. Every word is here pregnant with an intense life, a plenitude of meaning, and feelings that it is in a position to share with those who abandon themselves to its reverberations in recollection and attention.

It was surely inevitable that the prayer springing from the heart of the psalmist should express itself in a poetic word. And it was necessary that he himself be a poet. The Spirit of God came to create the prayer in his heart. And that the psalmist might in his turn diffuse the prayer, he would also become a creator, a *poiêtês*, in the strongest sense of the word "poet," that is, a "maker." For in this way each poet finds himself close to God, who created everything by his Word: he too is called to perfect creation by revealing, with the help of all the potential in his verse, the hidden and eternal meaning of the universe he sings.

To enter into the prayer of the Psalms is to be seized by the poetic and creative movement that issues forth from a psalm, a movement that proceeds not only from the spirit of an earthly poet but also—principally—from the Spirit of God who has taken hold of the poet. The spirit of a human being, even of a poet, knows only the depths of the human. But the Spirit of God, by contrast, scrutinizes all, even the depths of God. It is indeed this Spirit that we have received, "the Spirit that comes from God, that we might recognize the gifts that God has given us" (1 Cor 2:12). It is the same Spirit of which Paul says elsewhere that at the hour of prayer he comes to the aid of our weakness, since we know not how to pray as we ought and that it is he who, within us, intercedes for us with ineffable groanings (Rom 8:26). Thus, through the poetic word of the psalm, we are finally grasped by the Spirit of God and introduced into the prayer that he himself never ceases to place within our hearts.

Jesus the Psalmist

The prayer of Jesus arose in the same fashion. This prayer assumes a great importance for us since it is that of our high priest. In his humanity, he was called to restore the great liturgical dialogue that never ceased to unite heaven and earth before the fall of Adam, at the time when God still conversed familiarly with his first creatures.

The gospel frequently attests that Jesus prayed and that he prayed with the words of the Psalms. This prayer is not surprising if one recalls the essential bond of intimacy that, at the heart of the Trinity, unites the Word to his Father. It is only to be expected that this communion should come to expression in Jesus' prayer from the instant that the Word, becoming incarnate, took to itself a human nature. But if we reflect on the manner in which he prayed, a question arises. Was it necessary for Jesus to learn to pray, as for example he needed to learn obedience (Heb 5:8)? If we call to mind how one evangelist described Jesus' prayer with the imagery of struggle and agony (Luke 22:44), we need not hesitate to respond in the affirmative to this question. The humanity of Jesus was the same as ours, handicapped by the consequences of sin, over which he came to triumph. According to the New Testament, Jesus was able to be tempted just as we are, being like us in all things except sin (Heb 4:15). His heart must have experienced the difficulty of prayer just as his will was put to the test before submitting to the will of his Father (Luke 22:32). According to the very dynamic of the incarnation, however, Jesus was destined to become a fundamental and unique sign of prayer. He was called to reestablish prayer in a new manner that would endure to the end of time.

This prayer of Jesus was not bequeathed to him ready-made, nor did it come without pain. It formed part of the work of redemption. Jesus was to achieve it by a great struggle, as much in the first place on his own behalf as on ours afterward. The prayer of Jesus was therefore paschal and salvific. By means of this prayer, Jesus forges a path within his own human heart, a path in the heart of humanity through which the Word of God could penetrate so as to echo back praise to the Father in psalms and in prayer. To accomplish this, Jesus had to place himself in the school of the Psalms in union with the whole Jewish people and as head of the people of the New Covenant. He had to situate himself at the heart of the dynamism of the Spirit that animates the Psalms. Murmuring the Psalms and ruminating on them, his heart came to be wounded by them so that within this wound in his human heart, destined to become the source of a new prayer, the fullness of the Father's love might dwell and become manifest.

By coursing through the heart and mouth of Jesus, the Psalms took a decisive step. They issued forth re-created and transformed. Just as Jesus assumed the whole of human nature with its weaknesses that he might be in a position to save it in its integrity, in the same way he assimilated to himself the totality of the prayer of the Psalter so that, in the same words but through his very own heart, the marvel of Christian prayer might come to birth. Such prayer would henceforth beyond any doubt be acceptable to the Father because it expresses the full maturity of the adult human being in Christ.

Thus, in the prayer of Jesus, the poetic and creative power of God's Word in the Psalms attains a definitive fulfillment. It becomes a word of the new creation, an unceasing hymn of the new heavens and the new earth, a song of the heavenly liturgy, an echo on earth of the prayer of the high priest who continually celebrates and intercedes for us before the face of his Father (Heb 7:25).

Christian Prayer

It was through the Psalms prayed by Jesus that Christian prayer came to birth. In Jesus, a human heart became entirely transparent to the Word and was pervaded by it. The human heart of the Word of God became the natural receptacle of the Word, the interior temple from which this same Word was to spring forth in a new liturgy, from which the paschal prayer of the Church and of all humanity sounds forth unceasingly and forever. In the dialogue of the creature with its God, Jesus now opens a register of infinite holiness that only the Son himself can reveal. God is not only the Creator, the Lord of Hosts, the unshakable Rock and the Fortress of Salvation, such as he is worshiped in the Psalms, but also henceforth he is, in all simplicity, "the heavenly Father" whose astonishing proximity is offered us in Jesus.

This prayer is still marked by an explosion of praise and blessing before the marvels of salvation; but it does not merely commemorate past marvels in thanksgiving: it provokes and urges them forward (2 Pet 3:12) by the fervor it inspires: "Hallowed be thy name."

It also celebrates the definitive advent of the kingdom of God, already inaugurated in the passion and the resurrection of his Son and still awaiting consummation on that day when the entire universe will be subjected to him: "Thy kingdom come."

It already envisions the unobstructed unfolding of the love of God that fills the universe until his plan of mercy is fully accomplished: "Thy will be done."

It assumes intercession for all the needs of all people, that these may be met day by day in total dependence on a Father who gives to each one according to his or her necessities: "Give us this day our daily bread."

Humbly, it offers the same repentance that resounds through the whole Psalter in appeal and in abandonment to the mercy of God, yet now linked to the forgiveness and mercy that Jesus' new commandment establishes among believers: "Forgive us our trespasses, as we forgive those who trespass against us."

It again gives voice to the cry of distress before the trial that God sends to all his faithful ones and into which the Son has from now on victoriously preceded us: "Lead us not into temptation."

It empowers us to triumph over evil and over all enemy powers so that we can enter into the paschal triumph of Jesus, who has brought to conclusion all the curses of old by rendering them void: "But deliver us from evil."

Thus, the prayer that Jesus teaches his disciples after emerging from a night spent entirely in praise and intercession does no more than recover the same sentiments expressed by the psalmists of former days, all the while giving them new depth by his own experience as the Son. As an admirable abridgment that reduces the Jewish Psalter to its essential themes, the prayer to the Father enfolds and accompanies resoundingly the salvation that Jesus is on the point of bringing about, the salvation toward which all Christians are invited after him as they take up the same prayer in their hearts.

Learning to Pray

Oftentimes it's enough merely to meet one day a true man or woman of prayer for an irresistible desire to pray to emerge in oneself. There are many today, it seems, who carry this wound in their hearts, this obscure but insistent longing. Let us call it an attraction for prayer. It is an initial call of the Spirit in the heart of a believer that moves him to abandon himself to the mysterious current whose meaning and orientation are barely glimpsed. This attraction brings with it a certain facility for recollection, a spontaneous stripping-off of all that could distract from its activity, which takes place entirely in the interior depths.

But if true Christian prayer is to well up, it is not enough merely to give oneself up without discernment to this interior current. Jesus, our great high priest and psalmist, must still intervene in some fashion. The attraction must be recognized, identified, taken charge of by the spiritual power of the Word of God and, in particular, by that Word-made-prayer that is presented to us in the Psalter. All attraction for prayer will pass in some way through the Word of God before bringing together within us, unfailingly, the prayer of Jesus and the groaning of his Spirit. Prayer first passes through the sieve of the Word of God. In this way it is purified, but very quickly it is also taken in charge by this Word and animated by its vivifying breath, which comes forth from the very power of God. Thus, to every disciple asking how to pray, Jesus, even today, offers the Psalter.

The words of the Psalms come to meet the heart of the believer at the moment when the heart opens itself to prayer. This does not involve a purely intellectual process that would content itself with a rational analysis of the Psalter, whose themes would then be elaborated by a more profound reflection. We are dealing rather with a purely spiritual technique that the ancients knew under the name of *meletê* in Greek or *meditatio* in Latin. Now, it is the Psalter that was for them the object par excellence of this spiritual *meditatio*, meaning a slow rumination under the guidance of the Holy Spirit. It is urgent that we rediscover this technique today.

Such meditation responds, in part, to the demands of a poetic reading of the Psalter, something already indispensable at the level of the letter since this prayer is expressed in a highly poetic form. This holds all the more given that the poetic power of the Psalms, as we have already seen, is entirely at the service of the creative power of the Holy Spirit. Through the psalms the Spirit became the first poet of prayer.

To enter into the prayer of the Psalms a certain poetic reading proves indispensable. We must enter into harmony with the breath that created a psalm, the breath that continues to vibrate in its sounds, in the music of its syllables, in the rhythm of its words and verses, in the burst of its images. Only such harmonization can open us to the riches within a psalm. This raises the delicate problem of the translation of the Psalms into languages whose genius is inevitably foreign to the language of the Psalter.

The work of exegetes here reveals itself of capital importance. Their competence alone, however, does not suffice. For, where a psalm is concerned, its poetic reading coincides most of the time with its celebration in the liturgical assembly. In fact, many of the Psalms owe their origin to the cultural celebrations of ancient Israel. And Jesus himself, before making the Psalter the very fabric of his personal prayer, learned to know it at the assemblies of the synagogue or on the occasions of celebration at the Temple in Jerusalem. The poetry of the Psalms, in the majority of cases, cannot be adequately evaluated apart from its liturgical context. It presupposes a celebration.

The liturgical renewal has been sensitive to the unique character of each psalm and to the way in which its particular poetic weight can be enhanced through a celebration. And rightly so. In addition, the renewal has been largely inspired by the traditional techniques of psalmody that, in all the Churches and rites, has created a climate apt to release all the spiritual power of the words employed.

The principal characteristic of these techniques of psalmody consists in their manner of interiorizing the text. The evocative density of the symbols used by the psalmist is set in relief so as to promote and hasten a psalm's progressive descent into the depths of communal and individual consciousness. Liturgical celebration favors a collective rumination of the psalms that draws from them all the savor that nourishes the inner heart and makes it flower in silent jubilation before the Lord. By their very nature the Psalms have to be sung, and this sonorous language should be supported by certain gestures. Psalmodic cantilena is always discrete, however, its gesture very sober, limited to what is useful for its poetry—including its images, sounds, and rhythm—to deploy all its potential and gently imbue the heart of the one praying. Like all poetry, each psalm has its own strong "aroma," and it reaches and moves whoever lends it an ear.

In this way a psalm can be repeated unceasingly; it even begs to be repeated from the moment the heart is seized by the subtle incantation of its current of prayer. It is thus that the Psalms reverberate, in unending echoes, throughout the course of our days. One takes up a psalm as by instinct. It marks the passage of time: the night repeats it to the day and the hours reiterate it among themselves. Relays of prayer are thus spontaneously created throughout our days and nights as we endeavor unceasingly to transcend the passage of time and pass over into God's eternal present.

Indeed, it is already God's time that shines through the work of his Spirit in the psalms. For, if anyone abandons himself to this work, the poetic power of the Psalter causes him to enter into a divine rhythm, the rhythm of God, who breathes prayer into the human being. What heady power a psalm possesses, which can ravish its *poets* to the sober intoxication of prayer!

At a given moment of the celebration, the savor of a psalm reaches the heart of the one praying and merges with the incessant prayer that the Holy Spirit utters within him in ineffable groanings (Rom 8:26). At that instant, prayer is born in us. The words of the psalm connect with our heart, and this is the fruit of the poetic power of the Word of God that comes to us from the outside. But it is also the trace of the movement of the Spirit who, within our heart, reacts to the Word, recognizes it, makes it its own, and borrows its voice in order to burst forth exteriorly in an intercession that had until then been, quite literally, unutterable. At the moment when the two converge, irresistible prayer springs up within us. The psalm that had come to us from beyond ourselves becomes quite truly our own psalm. By means of the divinely poetic Word of the psalm, our heart has borne its fruit.

The Silence of Praise

This mystery reveals itself thanks to a certain quality of silence. That is why silence necessarily forms part of a spiritual technique of prayer. In addition, it has very naturally recovered its place even in the community celebrations of the postconciliar liturgy, where its role is essential. In this pause for a moment of rest within the flow of words, silence facilitates harmonization between the text of the psalm and the heart of the one praying. Silence is important to preserve all the psalm's density. It's not just a question of the absence of all exterior noise or even the suspension of all music; above all, the aim is to put a halt to all thoughts, images, and feelings likely to monopolize or redirect to themselves the spiritual energy of the Word. At such a moment, the time for conceptual analysis or logical reflection is past. In its place there has emerged a time for the peaceful rumination of the Word, in a stark attentiveness empty of concepts and desires, with the heart in a state of vigilance and profoundly docile to every impulse of the Spirit. We could speak of an interior "virginity" for which one could never pay too high a price, so indispensable is it to the process by which the Word imbues the heart and makes it bear fruit that endures.

Having arrived at this silence, one returns to the words of the psalm, but the prayer of the Psalter will now have been profoundly changed. The psalm is no longer offered only from the exterior, and effort is now scarcely required any more to enter into its substance. For it now issues from the interior, from the inner ground of the one praying. It is always the Holy Spirit, of course, who inspires the same words of the same psalm, but henceforward his breath blows through the flesh and the heart of the one praying. The substance of the psalm has become his own substance. He is a psalmist in his own right. He sings the psalm as if he were recomposing it, after the example of the great inspired figures of the Old Testament and of Jesus himself. He transcribes the Psalms into his own life, and all his experience can be translated into the Psalms. In a sense he is himself inspired, whether he is repeating the words of psalms already known or composing new ones, drawing, as did the Virgin at prayer, from the common fund of the tradition in the depths of her heart: "May the word of Christ dwell among you in all its richness . . . , singing to God in your hearts with thanksgiving, with psalms, with hymns, and with songs inspired by the Spirit" (Col 3:16).

It may be that the psalmist will return to his silence and even prefer to remain there. Perhaps that is what must happen at length. This evolution should not be surprising. With time, a multiplicity of words from the Psalter is no longer necessary. Not that these are now a burden; rather, they have already borne their fruit. They have been condensed into a few words, sometimes into a single but fundamental word, one of those words indefinitely ruminated on in which is summed up the entire good news of salvation and all the responses of the human person at prayer. From the "ten-stringed lute" (Ps 92:4) that it was at the beginning, the song of the prayer has become a lute of one string. This simplification cannot arrive at its complete fulfillment except in that sacred monotone that never ceases to propel us into "the one thing necessary": the tenderness of God.

Silence then becomes praise. And if any word still remains, it will be solely the Name of Jesus our Savior, the blessed and tirelessly invoked Name of him who exists entirely for the praise of God the Father (Phil 2:11).

11

The Word beyond the Liturgy

As soon as we raise the question of the true significance of liturgical action, we inevitably discover the Word of God, a reality that exceeds the liturgy all around, that precedes it as well as follows it, a reality of which the liturgy itself is the celebration. Announced in advance by the prophets (Acts 3:24), realized in its fullness by Christ, whom God has glorified by the power of his Spirit,[1] spread throughout the whole world by the apostolic preaching (Rom 10:17-18), attested by a multitude of witnesses and martyrs (Acts 5:41), the Word of God is proclaimed in the Church (1 Cor 11:26) and received in the heart of believers so as to bear fruit to eternal life.[2]

The whole of the Church's life and all her activity are absorbed in the spiritual event that is the *tradition*—that is, the "handing on"—of the Word:

> We announce to you the Eternal Life that was with the Father and has been manifested to us. What we have seen and heard, we also announce to you that you may have communion with us. For our communion is with the Father and with his Son Jesus Christ. And we are writing these things to you so that our joy may be complete. (1 John 1:2-4)

---

[1] See the innumerable texts of Saint John where Christ speaks of the work of the Father that he must accomplish. It is he who is the accomplishment of the promises made by God.

[2] See Matt 13:8; John 15:7-8. In connection with this paragraph, one may find it useful to reread the first two chapters of *Dei Verbum*, the Constitution on Divine Revelation of the Second Vatican Council: "Divine Revelation Itself" and "The Transmission of Divine Revelation."

Inaugurated in the liturgy, this tradition blossoms in many ways and constitutes the movement beyond the liturgy to which we now turn our reflections.

The Tradition of the Word

Although this "tradition" or handing-on of the Word embraces multiple aspects, nevertheless the work it pursues, the edifice it builds, and the spiritual reality it reveals are all one and the same thing.

The Word of God is above all the *apocalypse*, that is, the *revelation of the mystery*. Its mission is to unveil the hidden designs of God and thus to grant us entry into the mystery of the new creation. As the new human being in Christ, the Christian is constituted a child ("son") of God. He has received the anointing (1 John 2:27), the firstfruits of his inheritance, and the Spirit of adoption that makes him cry out: "Abba, Father!," thus bearing witness that he is truly a son of God (Rom 8:15, 23).

Such is the first aspect of the Word beyond the liturgical celebration. In welcoming the Word of God with faith, a person discovers, in awestruck surprise, his very identity as a son of God (1 John 3:1). The Word transforms him to such a degree that it places him before the face of God, thereby initiating the ineffable dialogue of interior prayer. Having long borne in his heart the transforming Word, the incorruptible seed of divine life (1 Pet 1:23), the human person, now a child of God, can return to his Father his Word in praise and prayer: *Eructavit cor meum verbum bonum*—"My heart hath uttered a good word!" (Ps 44:2, Douay).

Initiated in the very depths of the heart and stirred up unceasingly by the hearing of the Word in the ecclesial assembly, this spiritual liturgy flowers freely, whether in community or solitary celebration. But in both cases it is the same spiritual event that occurs by virtue of the "tradition" of the Word, whether we call it the inauguration of the new creation, the coming of the kingdom of God, or the parousia of the Lord.

Endowed with the power of the Spirit, the Christian is a sign at the very heart of the world, a seed of the world to come (Jas 1:18). He is himself a mystery in the Pauline sense of this word. For "it

pleased God to make all the fullness of the divinity to dwell cor-
poreally in Christ, and in him we are sharers in this fullness" (Eph
1:22-23), for "he is the head of his body, which is the Church: the
fullness of him who fills all things in every way" (Col 1:19; 2:9-10).

The Christian is therefore the kingdom of God present in this
world, but present in a hidden manner. The witness of his works
(Jas 2:18) as well as the witness of his lips that confess the Name
of Jesus (Heb 13:15; Rom 10:10) are ordered to the revelation of
the mystery that he himself is in the world. Such is the second
aspect of the Word beyond the liturgical celebration.

These two aspects have a common dynamism that leads both
of them to the definitive *beyond* that is nothing other than the
total revelation of the glory of God.

When the new creation has been brought to completion, when
the parousia of the Lord has come definitively, and when God
is known face to face just as he is, then once again the definitive
and renewing Word will be proclaimed in exultation and thanksgiving before the face of God and of all the Church gathered into
the kingdom from the farthest ends of the earth (*Didache* 9), and
that Word says: "Behold, I make all things new" (Rev 21:5; NAB).

The Teaching of the Council

With uncommon forcefulness, the constitution *Sacrosanctum
Concilium* affirms this reality we speak of, which, even while
transcending the liturgical action, gives it its full significance;
for, in the Church of God, "the human is directed toward and
subordinated to the divine, the visible to the invisible, action to
contemplation, and this present world to that city yet to come,
the object of our quest."[3] Thus, "in the earthly liturgy we take
part in a foretaste of that heavenly liturgy which is celebrated in
the holy city of Jerusalem toward which we journey as pilgrims,
where Christ is sitting at the right hand of God, minister of the
sanctuary and of the true tabernacle."[4]

---

[3] Second Vatican Council, *Sacrosanctum Concilium* (The Constitution on the
Sacred Liturgy) 2.

[4] *Sacrosanctum Concilium* 8.

In fact, "if we continue to love one another and to join in praising the Most Holy Trinity . . . we will be faithful to the deepest
vocation of the Church and will share in a foretaste of the liturgy
of perfect glory."[5]

In addition, the liturgy is not only the summit for which all the
activities of the Church prepare and toward which they converge;
it is also a wellspring from which every grace flows and especially "our sanctification in Christ and the glorification of God
to which all other activities of the church are directed, as toward
their end."[6] Without in any way diminishing the excellence of the
liturgical celebration, however, it is necessary also to recall that
"the spiritual life . . . is not limited solely to participation in the
liturgy."[7] Prayer in common cannot render void the value of the
spiritual liturgy that is celebrated in the inner room, according
to gospel testimony (Matt 6:6). This is the interior and hidden
spiritual liturgy that ought to blossom into continuous prayer,
according to the precept of the Apostle (1 Thess 5:17) and the rec-
ommendation of the whole tradition. Beginning with the spiritual
sacrifice celebrated in community, the liturgy consecrates us to
be a *munus aeternum*, an eternal offering. It teaches us "always
carry around in our bodies the dying of Jesus, so that the life too
of Jesus may be made manifest in our mortal flesh."[8]

Therefore, it is not without a certain insistence that the council
fathers wished to recall what lies beyond the liturgical celebration: both the heavenly liturgy, in which we already participate,
and interior prayer, the true spiritual liturgy that is the very expression of the gift of self to the Lord through conformity to
his death and resurrection. This insistence, for all its discretion,
occasions a certain difficulty, namely, the need to specify the
relationship between liturgy and Christian experience, liturgy
and *kerygma*, liturgy and mysticism. The discovery of the values

---

[5] Second Vatican Council, *Lumen Gentium* (The Dogmatic Constitution on
the Church) 51; in both cases, the text reads: *praegustando participamus* ("we par-
take [of it] by way of a foretaste").

[6] *Sacrosanctum Concilium* 10.

[7] *Sacrosanctum Concilium* 12.

[8] *Sacrosanctum Concilium* 12, citing 2 Cor 4:10-11.

that are displayed at the very heart of the liturgical celebration could at times block the perception of a deeper reality, present at the core of the liturgical action: I speak of the spiritual experience that infuses life, simultaneously, into the liturgy, interior prayer, and apostolic ministry. In fact, these diverse manifestations of the same spiritual experience convey the same life, the life of the Spirit given to the Church and transmitted by the Church through her faith.

Hence the liturgy is the original cell, the kernel, the seed from which all the life of the Church spreads out ever more widely. In a certain sense, the Church and the liturgy coincide: all the ecclesial *energies* are contained in the liturgical celebration. In every person and in every community, therefore, there will be a necessary continuity between the liturgy and all that lies *beyond* it. The latter will have no value except in the measure that it is guaranteed the perpetual mutual influence between the liturgical source and what we have called its *plerôma*: the fullness of its reality beyond the texts and the rites, that is, the Spirit within us expressing himself in prayer and witness, the Spirit that groans within us in anticipation of the fullness of redemption when we will be introduced into the "city of the great king."

By an exercise in continual transcendence, every celebration must lead us back to this *reality beyond*, the full reality that is also the center of the liturgical mystery. Such an impulse to go beyond the immediate brings about a simplification of the liturgical rites. Thus, by means of unencumbered rites that are transparent to the mystery of life they express and communicate, the Christian people participate fully and actively in the holy liturgy, exercising the royal priesthood with which it is invested by its baptism.[9]

Monasticism: A Work of God

For anyone who reads the ancient monastic texts without being distracted by any modern problematic, the vital link that ties the

---

[9] See *Sacrosanctum Concilium* 14.

liturgy to its *beyond* is clearly apparent, the sign of a robust spiritual health. Problems generally do not arise with this mode of reading, for one and the same life animates all the manifestations of the one mystery. The only concern is to remain in the Word, taking care that no sterile human eloquence should quench the Spirit in human hearts.

Many are the testimonies that could be cited to bring to light this harmonious interpenetration of liturgy, prayer, and monastic life. We will consider several examples. Suffice it for the moment to recall the curious but suggestive semantic evolution of the expression *opus Dei*.[10] In the most ancient texts, the "work of God" designates the whole spiritual life of the monk and, more simply, monastic life as such. Progressively the phrase came to designate almost exclusively the life of prayer organized around the reading of the Word, psalmody, and silent prayer.

In later texts, in the Rule of Saint Benedict for example, the expression is reserved for the liturgical celebration. The strong and global sense is not, however, totally abandoned. When Saint Benedict speaks of the *opus Dei*, he means by this, first of all, the communal celebration. He does not, however, exclude what we are here calling its *beyond*, which for a monk manifests itself especially in the spiritual liturgy that is the prayer of the heart. The latter is learned in the communal celebration. It is there that the young monk strives to recover the *place of the heart*, the living sanctuary of the spiritual liturgy.[11] The liturgical celebration and the interior liturgy, in perpetual reference to each other, constitute the heart of monastic life to such an extent that both are called, by curious antonomasia, by the same name: *opus Dei*.

---

[10] See Irénée Hausherr, "*Opus Dei*," *Orientalia Christiana Periodica* 13 (1947): 195–218; reprinted in *Études de spiritualité orientale* (Rome: Typis Pontificiae Universitatis Gregorianae, 1969), 121–44.

[11] "The heart free of thoughts and moved by the Spirit is a true sanctuary, even before entering into the future condition of heaven. Here all is celebrated and expressed spiritually. Whoever has not yet attained this state can, through his other virtues, be a stone fit for building up the temple of God, but he is not the temple of the Spirit or its pontiff." Gregory of Sinai, *On the Commandments*, 7.

"Prefer nothing to the work of God," says Saint Benedict.[12] By this he does not intend, however, to establish a preference for liturgical prayer over interior prayer but rather means that the activity of prayer, whether personal or communal, is the essence of monastic life. In this, he faithfully echoes the most authentic monastic tradition: "A measure has not been indicated, for to say 'Pray always and without ceasing' does not propose any measure. Indeed, the monk who prays only when he is standing at prayer, does not pray at all."[13]

The Mystery of the Word

The organic link that exists, on the one hand, between monastic life and the *opus Dei*, and on the other hand, within the work of God between the liturgical celebration and its *beyond*, rests on a kinship of structure. This common structure takes shape around the Word of God and its mystery within us, around what we called at the beginning *the tradition of the Word*.

It is a mystery of prodigious efficacy, this Word that does not depart from the mouth of God only to return to him void, with-

---

[12] RB 43.3.

[13] *Par questions et réponses, sur la façon dont il faut demeurer dans sa cellule et sur la contemplation*, n. 9, in *Apophthegmes des Pères du desert*, trad. J.-C. Guy (Textes de la Spiritualité Orientale, n. 1), ms. (Bégrolles-en-Mauges, Abbaye de Bellefontaine), 422. See B. Besret, "Célébration de l'office et vie spirituelle," in: *La Maison Dieu* 88 (1966): 83–95. The author insists on the kinship between spiritual life and liturgy: "Between them a progressive osmosis must take place, establishing a growing homogeneity to the point that the passage from one to the other can scarcely be felt. The office then becomes the communal form of my prayer, but before, during, and after it is the same spiritual life that is pursued." See also P. Deseille, "La formation liturgique dans les monastères," *Liturgie et monastère* (1967): 140: "It is not a matter of suppressing private prayer and granting to the liturgy a monopoly. Nothing could be more opposed to the practice of the ancient monks, who knew that liturgical celebrations cannot themselves become an interior prayer unless they are prepared and prolonged in moments devoted to private prayer or, more precisely, to what medieval monasticism called 'spiritual exercises': that is, the contemplative reading of biblical and patristic texts; the savory rumination of texts learned by heart during *meditation*; elevations of the heart to God in prayers that are brief and frequent and take up the formulas of Scripture in a personal mode, thus leading to abiding in silence before God."

out having accomplished his will and completed its mission (Isa 55:10-11).

It is within the heart that a human being must embrace the Word of God. Restored to its original integrity, the human heart is made for the Word and the Word is made for the human heart. It is in the heart that the Word is sown (Matt 13:19; Luke 8:12). But this heart must be purified (Matt 5:8; Heb 10:22) and well disposed (Luke 8:15), for our heart is habitually hardened and our spirit closed off (Mark 6:52; 8:17; John 12:40; Eph 4:18; Heb 3:8; 15; 4:7). It is slow to give itself to the Word (Luke 24:25). It is full of shadows (Rom 1:21). It is easily weighed down with pleasures and anxieties (Luke 21:34). For these reasons the heart thus becomes incapable of tasting its spiritual food, which is the Word of God.

That is why God himself must intervene to open the human heart, to remove from our bodies the heart of stone and give us a heart of flesh (Ezek 36:26-27), so that once again we may devote ourselves to the Word (Acts 16:14).

The Lord Jesus broke the bread of the Word for us so that at his voice our hearts might ignite and burn within us (Luke 24:32), so that the eyes of our heart might be completely enlightened (Eph 1:18). After ascending to the Father, he sent us another Paraclete (John 14:16): the Anointing that teaches us everything (1 John 2:27), the Holy Spirit who reminds us of all Christ said to us (John 14:26).

In this way the Word is, so to speak, handed over to the human heart. A fertile and life-giving dialogue is started between the Spirit who was slumbering in the depths of our heart and the Spirit who rises up in the Word. Brought forth anew from an incorruptible seed (1 Pet 1:23), the heart is reborn from the Word. In the Word we recognize the new countenance of our rebirth in Christ (Jas 1:23); "the hidden person of the heart" (1 Pet 3:4) takes shape and consistency within us.

Both the Old and New Testaments use a very rich vocabulary in describing this fundamental operation by which the Word of God invests the human heart, is assimilated by it and—through this heart made new—is returned to God. The heart welcomes the Word, consumes and digests it (Ezek 3:1-3). The human being hides it in his heart (Ps 118:11), shelters it in his bosom (Job 23:12), keeps it (Luke 8:15), explores it (Ps 118:2, 24, 69, 115), devotes himself to it (Acts 16:14), ponders it within himself (Luke 2:19), and murmurs it day and night (Ps 1:2). He abides unceasingly in the Word and makes his dwelling in it (John 8:31), just as the Word abides and dwells in him (Col 3:16).

Once transformed by it, the heart can return the Word (*eructare Verbum*: "utter the Word," Ps 44:2). The Word has now become the treasury of the heart (Luke 6:45) from which the father of the family knows how to bring forth both the new and the old (Matt 13:52). Abounding in thanksgiving (Col 2:7), the heart is consecrated as a sanctuary of perpetual prayer and Eucharist.

Henceforth the heart has recovered the activity for which it was made, which consists of turning the Word over and over again within itself. Cassian calls it the *volutatio cordis* or "rolling of the heart."[14] Our heart becomes completely imbued with the Word, *anima gravida Verbi*, as Saint Bernard says: "a soul pregnant with the Word."[15]

The heart is now ready to send back the Word of God, to offer it anew in the Spirit, to become a witness and testimony before one's brothers, to become praise and intercession before God.

We have therefore rediscovered in the Word of God, in the spiritual event and its "tradition," the unifying principle of every work of prayer within us. This "progress of the Word" (2 Thess 3:1) orders the structures that culminate in an ineffable dialogue between the Word and our heart.

Instead of restricting ourselves to a scriptural terminology, we could have described the same process by means of the spiritual vocabulary of East and West.[16] For here we are touching on a constant of the spiritual—and especially monastic—literature

---

[14] *Conferences* 10.13.

[15] *Sermons on the Song of Songs* 65.13.

[16] In the East: *anagignóskein, apostethízein, epikaleín, mnêmê, kryptê, ergasía, kryptê melêtê, hê entós ergasía, ergasía Theoû*, and so on (see I. Hausherr, *Noms du Christ et voies d'oraison* [Rome: Pontificium Institutum Orientalium Studiorum, 1960]). In the West: *lectio, meditatio, ruminatio, volutatio, reditus ad cor, dulcis me-*

of all ages, of every region and in all milieus, whether cenobitic or eremitical.

And now, by examining some examples from the immense monastic patrimony, I would like to stress the universality of this spiritual experience of the Word of God. This brief survey will be terribly limited. Nevertheless, we would like it to be as suggestive as possible.

The Book of Steps: The Three Churches

The first document for us to examine, *Liber Graduum* (*The Book of Steps*),[17] derives from Asia Minor. Contemporary with the origins of monasticism, to which it seems to make an allusion, this very ancient writing is testimony to a premonastic tradition.

The author addresses some ascetics who may or may not form a group. Although they are Christians who want to live in the state of perfection, they do not habitually keep themselves apart from the Christian community. Their way of life is naturally itinerant. Nonetheless, they frequent the liturgical celebrations common to all. They are in a special way devoted to prayer and teaching.

Written in the Syriac language, this document presents a complete exposition of spiritual theology based on a vision of God and humanity drawn directly from the Bible. The Jewish Christian

---

moria, otium, quies (see J. Leclercq, *Otia monastica: Études sur le vocabulaire de la contemplation au Moyen Âge* [Rome: Herder, 1963]).

[17] Edited by M. Kmosko in 1926 in the *Patrologia Syriaca*, 1, 3, the *Liber Graduum* or "The Book of Steps" was dated by him to the beginning of the 320s, very early after the end of the persecutions, in the Syria under Roman jurisdiction. This date has since been contested in favor of a later date, but it seems one may retain it as the most probable. The spirituality of these homilies is clearly premonastic. The author is suspicious of an unusual spiritual movement that has recently appeared in his Church and that induces some of her members to separate from her in order to pray in a more intense way that does not correspond with the received usages (*Liber Graduum* 27.5). To do so, certain Christians "separate themselves from the Church and go off to the mountain" (12.4). This last expression designates monastic withdrawal in the most ancient Syriac documents. One is tempted to wonder if this document is not the most ancient witness to the first monastic migrations in Mesopotamia in the early fourth century.

subsoil is often apparent. Despite its antiquity, *The Book of Steps* developed from early on a theology of the relationship between liturgy and interior prayer.

God destined the human person to be, in his or her heart, a *liturgical being*. Being mysteriously present both in heaven and on earth as a living link between the visible and the invisible creation, Adam was "holy and perfect in the manner of watchers and angels while remaining on earth in his body. Entirely stripped of what is earthly, however, he lived in spirit in heaven with the angels, his spirit being adorned with the glory of his creator."[18]

Adam did not maintain himself in this state, and his role as cosmic liturgist was consequently disrupted. The whole of his being became earthly. Henceforth he would have to content himself with a mere shadow of the genuine good for which he had been destined. Instead of being clothed with the glory of God, he would cover himself with clothes sewn by human hands. In place of the bread of angels, he would nourish himself on bread gotten by the sweat of his brow. Rather than with the society of angels, he would have to be satisfied with the community of marriage and home.[19]

These earthly images of true, lasting goods are not bad in themselves but, for the author of *The Book of Steps*, they do not correspond to God's primordial design. They remain oriented toward a *beyond* and their goal is to redirect humanity to communion with the true goods.

The liturgy is one of the aspects of this economy by which humanity is led back to its true home in the heavens. It is by journeying through a sensible and corporeal liturgy that the Christian rediscovers his heavenly citizenship. This journey will demand that he die to things below in order to allow Christ, the second Adam, to increase in him.

This "return to heaven" in no way disdains common prayer, whose rites are inevitably corporeal. These rites always remain a necessary passage, impossible to avoid. Before arriving at spiritual

---

[18] *Liber Graduum* (hereafter LG) 21.2.
[19] LG 21.10.

prayer, it is first essential to "offer sacrifice" as is done habitually in the Churches: "sometimes standing erect, at other times prostrating on one's knees, then processing or singing in the Holy Spirit."[20] Even musical instruments have their own value for prayer. They bring aid to those who do not yet know how to "play on the lyres and harps of the Spirit," nor how to "praise the Lord with their interior senses."[21]

This liturgical prayer, celebrated at determined times, comes to full flower in the continual prayer of the perfect. This prayer is a distinctive trait of those whom the author is addressing.[22] It is called "prayer at all times," "continual prayer," "praise," "confession," "continual meditation on the Lord," "sacrifice of the heart,"[23] "hidden prayer of the heart that clings to the Lord and thinks of him without ceasing."[24] All visible liturgy must therefore end in this invisible liturgy of the heart. The latter, in turn, leads to the heavenly liturgy. The question here is of a concrete aspect of this economy that leads from the visible to the invisible. We note that the vocabulary is still entirely biblical, without Platonic influence:

> God has made two worlds and two liturgies, so that from the visible liturgy the invisible might be manifested. Thus the visible Covenant is comparable to the hidden Covenant, as visible prayer is to hidden prayer, and the visible sacrifice to the hidden sacrifice, and the visible charisms to the hidden charisms.

---

[20] LG 27.5; this whole passage is directed against a whimsical teaching that claims to initiate one into prayer without reference to "the Church and her priests."

[21] LG 7.6; literally: "with the members," which generally designates the human heart, spirit, and voice; this "voice" is essentially spiritual, related as it is to the Spirit and to the Word. *The Book of Steps* is therefore more tolerant and less spiritualistic than Clement of Alexandria, who explicitly forbids the use of musical instruments in Christian worship; see *Pedagogy* 2.4.

[22] See LG 7.20; 14.2: "The just possess one or two doors in heaven and there they knock five times a day. But for the perfect, heaven is all doors before them. All the day long they contemplate the Lord, confessing and praising him, progressing from glory to glory in the Spirit, and contemplating the Lord in their heart as in a mirror."

[23] LG 3.14.

[24] LG 12.1.

> In a word, the liturgy on earth is entirely comparable to the one in the heavens. Thus, those who abide in the visible Church and eat of the visible sacrifice are living in the hidden Church in heaven and eat from the hidden altar in heaven: it is an ineffable liturgy that surpasses all human expression![25]

This capital text affirms forcibly the link that binds every celebration here below with its corresponding *beyond*. From this *beyond*, furthermore, it receives all its substance. For the visible liturgy was instituted by Moses. In the face-to-face vision that God accorded him on the summit of Mount Sinai, Moses was initiated "to serve God by the Spirit in heaven" just as Adam had done prior to his fall. Moses could therefore, on the strength of his spiritual experience, show to the people "in a corporeal manner the whole liturgy of the Spirit." Starting with him, the earthly liturgy once again participates in the liturgy of heaven.[26]

The complete passage from one liturgy to the other is accomplished in three steps or, according to the vocabulary of the author, by passing through three "Churches": that of the community, that of the heart, and finally that of heaven:

> The Church here below, her altar and her baptism, gives birth to people as nurslings. She suckles them with milk until the time of weaning. But when they begin to grow . . . they make temples of their bodies and altars of their hearts while eating a better and more solid food than milk, until they become perfect and eat of the Lord himself in all truth, just as he said: "The one who eats of me will live because of me. . . . These will attain to the Church on high that makes them perfect, they will enter into the city of Jesus, our king, and will serve in the great and excellent palace that is the mother of all the living.[27]

None of these three steps can be neglected. The author often insists on this; each step has its own time and function:

[25] LG 28.8.
[26] LG 28.10.
[27] LG 12.3.

If we disdain this visible Church and if we separate ourselves from her and from her visible altar, from the visible priesthood and from the baptism that purifies, our body will never become a temple nor will our heart become an altar and a fountain of praise. The Church above, her altar, her light, and her priesthood would likewise not be revealed to us. There all the saints are gathered, those who have a pure heart and live in glory and rejoice in the light, because they have not despised this blessed educator that every day gives birth and instructs.[28]

At the midpoint, like an intermediate step between the Church below and the Church above, the author locates "the Church of the heart" where the interior liturgy is celebrated invisibly, "the invisible work of the one who has known his own heart,"[29] who knows how the heart "celebrates as a priest interiorly."[30] It is to this Church that, in the first instance, the visible liturgy must lead. She is the meeting place of the liturgy here below and the celestial liturgy.

The celestial liturgy was the portion for which God had destined Adam:

Spend your life in this way: with your spirit, be in heaven like a citizen of the celestial heights, and with your body be on earth like a pilgrim and a foreigner. But let your liturgy be on high. Offer your praises in the manner of a watcher (angel) among other watchers.[31]

One sees here the point to which the presence of the mystery within the liturgical rites is conceived in a dynamic way. There is not an immediate and total coincidence, a perfect identity between the gesture and the mystery, but rather a progressive initiation and an ever greater openness toward an interior and heavenly reality that is, moreover, present from the beginning.

[28] LG 12.2.
[29] LG 12.6.
[30] LG 12.2.
[31] LG 21.3.

One could speak properly here of an inchoate presence, called to a continual deepening beyond the rite. Besides, the continuity between the three Churches and their liturgies becomes evident. It is found in the Spirit and in the power of his activity. It is, in fact, the same Spirit that works unceasingly, adapting his *liturgical action* to the spiritual capacity of Christians:

> It's not that the wet-nurse lacks the means of feeding her children, but rather that the children cannot tolerate solid food. The Spirit who celebrates in the visible Church is not less powerful than the one who celebrates in the Church of the heart or in the Church on high, for it is the same Spirit who celebrates in the three Churches. But the sons of Adam are very weak and it is first of all necessary to feed them like nurslings.[32]

Saint John Cassian and Saint Benedict

From this ancient and premonastic tradition, we pass to a cenobitic milieu already strongly structured: the monastic traditions of Southern Gaul and Italy, one or two centuries later. The uncontested master here is Saint John Cassian.

Formed in monastic life at two semieremitical centers of Lower Egypt, Cassian remained in his deepest heart a disciple of the famous Desert Fathers. One might entertain suspicions regarding the objectivity of his testimony, but one can doubt neither his sincerity nor his personal genius nor, above all, his decisive influence in the sphere of prayer and liturgy in Western monasticism.

In the second book of his *Institutes*, Cassian endeavors to promote a liturgical reform in the monasteries of Gaul, a reform in favor of greater contemplative interiority, by diminishing the number of psalms, maintaining with particular care the pauses for contemplative prayer,[33] and not paying attention to the number of verses recited but rather to the spiritual insight one draws from them.[34]

---

[32] LG 12.5.
[33] John Cassian, *Institutes* 2.7.10.
[34] *Institutes* 2.11.

This lightening of the Office does not aim merely at eliciting the greatest spiritual profit from the celebration itself. It is also intended to free the monk for the interior liturgy: "This modest number of obligatory prayers has been divinely measured to reserve for those whose faith is ardent the time to pursue their tireless course."[35] As soon as the Office is over, everyone hastens to his cell where he once again offers prayer, alone or with another brother, still more attentively, as a private sacrifice.[36] In the prolongation of canonical vigils, one celebrates private vigils with renewed care.[37] Private vigils do not differ from communal celebrations as regards their object. Both consist of a succession of psalms (*psalmi*) that are listened to or recited and of silent prayers (*orationes*). Both bear the same name: *opus nocturnum* or *meditatio*.[38]

This interior celebration is prolonged throughout the day. It is accompanied by manual work adapted so as to facilitate silent prayer and abolish its restriction to designated time periods.[39] In Egypt, the monks excel in this celebration of the heart. They can also, Cassian explains, dispense with the recitation of the little hours whose usage had spread into Syria and Mesopotamia and that Cassian had discretely recommended to the monks of Gaul. The monks of Egypt never interrupt the "meditation of the psalms and the other Scriptures, which they mix at every moment into prayers and orisons." In so doing, "they spend the whole day in liturgies that we ourselves celebrate only at determined times."[40]

One can see the clear continuity that Cassian establishes between communal celebration and its *beyond*, the interior liturgy. This latter is intended to prolong the canonical liturgy and ensure its total fruition. At times the interior liturgy will even replace the canonical liturgy, for "what is offered without interruption

---

[35] *Institutes* 2.12.2.
[36] *Institutes* 2.12.3.
[37] *Institutes* 2.13.3.
[38] *Institutes* 2.12.3.
[39] *Ita ne meditationi quidem spirituali finis imponatur* (*Institutes* 2.14).
[40] *Institutes* 3.2.

is more valuable than what is accomplished at fixed times, and a voluntary gift is more agreeable than actions accomplished by a regular summons."[41] This possible substitution does not pose any problem, and Cassian is inclined to see in it only advantages. For the schemas of the two celebrations are exactly the same: *psalmodia* or *scriptura*, that is, psalms and Scripture, and *oratio* or *preces*, that is, personal prayers, all of which together form the *meditatio spiritualis*.

This *meditatio* tends to become the sole occupation of the monk, the *iugis meditatio* ("perpetual meditation") or *usus incessabilis* ("incessant practice")[42] on a Word of God leading the heart to pure prayer.[43] Here one may recall the celebrated passage where Cassian describes the spiritual comprehension of the Scriptures and the manner in which the Psalms become the nourishment of prayer.

Saint Benedict uses even more faithfully the technical vocabulary of Saint John Cassian and seems well acquainted with a situation that is analogous in every respect.[44] For both the Word (*psalmodia, lectio*) and for prayer (*oratio*) he envisages a double celebration: the one public, the other private.

Alongside the communal psalmody considered down to its details, the Rule recommends the private praying of the Psalter, to which can be joined the reading of Scripture.[45] Saint Benedict designates this practice by the name he inherited from Cassian: *meditatio*—the interior and spiritual rumination of the Psalms. It hardly differs from the meditative reading of Scripture, with which it is often associated besides.[46] The same term sums up

---

[41] *Institutes* 3.2.

[42] *Conferences* 10.11.

[43] *Conferences* 10.11.

[44] See A. de Vogüé, "Le sens de l'Office divin d'après la règle de saint Benoît," *Revue d'ascétique et de mystique* 42 (1966): 389–404; 43 (1967): 21–23. We think, however, that while the proclamation or rumination of the Psalter certainly constitutes an indispensable way to interior prayer, it is already a true prayer in itself.

[45] RB 48.13: *Vacent lecitonibus suis aut psalmis* ("Let them devote their time to their reading or to the Psalms").

[46] RB 48.23: *meditari aut legere* ("to meditate or to read").

once again all the disciplines of monastic initiation: the *meditatio* is the principal occupation of the novice.[47]

As with the monks of Egypt described by Cassian, the interval that follows night prayer is, by preference, devoted to this meditation: *Quod vero restat post vigilias, a fratribus qui psalterii vel lectionum aliquid indigent, meditationi inserviatur*: "The time remaining after Vigils should be devoted to meditation by those who want something of the psalter or the readings."[48] This sentence, perfectly clear to anyone who knows the technical vocabulary of John Cassian's *Institutes*, has been very badly translated and interpreted by the majority of modern commentators. The word *indigere* signifies for these a need for intellectual studies, to which they reduce the *meditatio*.[49] Yet there can be no doubt that *meditatio* retains here, more than ever, its strict sense: the interior and private rumination of the Psalter and Scripture. As for the verb *indigere*, it means not only a need to be supplied but also, more positively, the interior attraction that moves the monk to this solitary meditation.[50]

---

[47] RB 58.

[48] RB 8.3.

[49] Here are several examples. Antoine Calmet: "For the time that remains after the night office, they apply themselves to learning the Psalms and the lessons of which they will have need" (*Commentaire littéral historique et moral sur la règle de Saint Benoît*. Paris, 1734; 2nd ed., 1847); Benedictines of Farnborough: "Let the brothers who are lacking in knowledge of the Psalms and the lessons devote this time to study" (Paris, 1914); Augustin Savaton: "The time that remains after Vigils, the brothers shall employ, according to need, to the study of the Psalter or the lessons" (*La Règle bénédictine commentée*. Paris, 1914); Gregorio Penco: "The interval that then remains after Vigils should be used by the monks to learn the Psalter or the lessons contained in their reading" (*Sancti Benedicti Regula*: introduzione, testo, apparati, traduzione e commento a cura di G. Penco [Firenze: La Nuova Italia, 1958]); Antoine Dumas: "It will be employed for study by the brothers who need to learn something of the Psalter or of the lessons" (*La Règle de saint Benoît*; Coll. Foi vivante. Paris: Cerf, 1961); E. de Solms: "What remains of the time will be devoted to the study of the Psalter or of the lessons by those brothers who have need thereof" (*La Vie et la règle de saint Benoît*. Paris: Desclée de Brouwer, 1965).

[50] Thus *indigens* can have the meaning of "one who desires": see Blaise-Chirat, *Dictionnaire du latin chrétien* (Turnhout: Brepols, 1954). *Indigentia carnalis* designates carnal desire, according to Saint Augustine (*De Sermone Domini in Monte* 1.15.42).

The meaning of the passage now becomes clear. Saint Benedict invites the brothers to give themselves to private meditation during the time that separates the end of Vigils from the break of day, at least those who *psalterii vel lectionum aliquid indigent*: those who feel *attracted*, who *feel* the need to pray the Psalms or to do a bit of reading. This phrase does not envision an intellectual preparation for the liturgical celebration; rather, it describes its *beyond* in a private celebration to which all freedom must be granted.

It is necessary to make the same assertion for the *oratio* of which the Rule speaks. It too becomes twofold. The first instance takes place *in conventu*, at the liturgical *synaxis* celebrated in common. It should be brief: at the signal of the superior, all the brothers rise together.[51] The allusion is crystal clear to the *orationes* spoken of by Cassian, those moments of silent prayer at the end of each psalm according to the practice of the monks of Egypt.[52] Saint Benedict must have been aware of this practice of having an *oratio* at the end of each psalm.[53]

The other *oratio* of which Saint Benedict speaks took place, strictly speaking, outside any liturgical celebration, once the work of God was finished (*expleto opere Dei*).[54] It is called private or *peculiaris*.[55] It permits one to pray *secretius* ("in private or apart")[56] or, again, *simpliciter*, that is to say, "in solitude, alone."[57] That is why Saint Benedict recommends that, outside the time of the office, the oratory be a place of silence and recollection.

---

[51] RB 20.

[52] *Institutes* 2.73: *omnes pariter eriguntur* ("all rise together").

[53] See RB 67, where it is a question of the "final prayer of the work of God," which supposes that there would have been several such prayers.

[54] RB 52.2.

[55] RB 49.5 and 52.3-4. The word still retains in the Rule of Saint Benedict the etymological sense of "savings that one possesses in one's own right": see RB 55.2.

[56] See Tertullian, *De oratione* 1, and Cyprian, *De dominica oratione* 4, for the expression *secrete orare* as specifically designating private prayer as opposed to that celebrated in common.

[57] RB 52.4. Not "in all simplicity," as it is often understood. The primary sense of *simpliciter* is "alone," "by oneself."

This private prayer will generally be brief so as to be pure,[58] according to an order borrowed from Saint John Cassian.[59] It can be prolonged, however, in keeping with the action of grace. To the *indigentia*, the interior desire that commands the private recitation of the Psalter, there corresponds an *inspiratio* of grace that leads the monk to prolong his personal prayer. But in general, a brief prayer, fervent and often repeated, is the most secure path toward the state of continual prayer. Already John Cassian counseled to "make brief but very frequent prayers: frequent so that we may, in praying more often to God, adhere constantly to him; brief so as to evade by this means the arrows with which the devil attacks us and tries to conquer us, above all at the time of prayer."[60] These prayers will guide us to the continual prayer that Saint Benedict cites among the instruments of good works, after the hearing of the Word of God: *Lectiones sanctas libentes audire, orationi frequenter incumbere* ("Listen readily to holy reading and devote yourself often to prayer").[61] The order of exercises here is meaningful. It underscores very discreetly the link that unites the Word to prayer.[62]

Barsanuphius, John of Gaza, and Hesychasm

We now come to another tradition, that of Palestinian *hesychasm*. Our witnesses are two old men of whom we know nothing except

---

[58] See RB 20.

[59] *Institutes* 2.10.3.

[60] *Institutes* 2.10.3.

[61] RB 4.55-56.

[62] A. de Vogüé ("Orationi frequenter incumbere," in *Revue d'ascétique et de mystique* 41 [1965]: 467–72) has shown that the expression *frequens oratio* was in that era a synonym of *iugis oratio*, "continual prayer." Innumerable texts of the monastic tradition describe the sweetness of the "private vigils" that follow the celebration of the liturgy. The Cistercian Gilbert of Hoyland (twelfth century) describes as follows the silent, solitary, and fervent prayer that occupies the night hours, of which Vigils are only the firstfruits (*quaedam primitiae*): "This prayer, borne by a pure affection, does not merely issue in words. Love makes itself heard in the ears of the Lord. It has no need of the noise of words which, while they may stir up the beginner, nevertheless disturb the one who prays perfectly" (G. of Hoyland, *Homily on the Canticle* 23.3; PL 184.120).

that they lived as recluses at the beginning of the sixth century in the monastery of Abba Seridos in southern Gaza. They are Barsanuphius, the Great Elder, and John of Gaza, "the Prophet."

With its distinctly eremitical orientation, the *hesychastic* tradition develops a very interiorized spirituality that, at first glance, leaves little room for the communal celebration of the liturgy. And with good reason! Among hermits and recluses, common prayer is almost nonexistent. Yet paradoxically, it is perhaps here that we will be able to grasp with the utmost clarity the fundamental identity of structure that binds the liturgy and its *beyond*.

For the monk who has installed himself in *hesychia* and has embraced the eremitical life, only one thing matters: to clutch firmly the sword of the Spirit, that is, the *diakrisis* (discernment) that is the spiritual instrument permitting the hermit to recognize in his own heart the promptings of the Spirit. It is these impulses that regulate the life of the hesychast, thus replacing the canons or regulations that organize life in the *cenobium*:

> A hesychast . . . possesses no rule. On the contrary, where you are concerned, you are to do like the man who eats and drinks in the measure he finds most agreeable. Thus, when you apply yourself to reading and notice compunction arising in your heart, then read with all your being. The same applies to psalmody. As for thanksgiving and litanies, embrace them according to your strength and without fear: the graces of God are without repentance![63]

Along the same lines we read:

> Therefore, do not desire prescriptions, for I do not wish you to be under the law, but under grace. It is said, in fact: "For the just, no law is imposed," and we desire that you be among the just. Hold fast to discernment as the pilot who directs the ship in the face of the wind.[64]

---

[63] Barsanuphius and John of Gaza, Letter 88. All the texts of Barsanuphius and John of Gaza are extracts from the edition of Nicodemus of the Holy Mountain (reedited in Athens in 1960), accessible in tomes 426–27 and 450–51 of *Sources chrétiennes* (Paris: Éditions du Cerf, 1998 and 2000).

[64] Barsanuphius and John of Gaza, Letter 23.

Such, then, is the activity of the hermit, entirely directed by the Spirit in keeping with the witness of the Apostle (Rom 8:14).

And if the Spirit of God is thus the rule and the canon of everything, it will certainly be so in regard to prayer. To a monk who asks him about the right measure of incessant prayer and whether he must follow a rule concerning this subject, Barsanuphius replies:

> The measure of unceasing prayer belongs to *apatheia*.[65] When you have known the coming of the Spirit, it will teach you all things. If it teaches you all things, it will also teach you in the matter of prayer. For the Apostle has said: "We do not know how to pray as we ought, but the Spirit himself intercedes for us with ineffable groaning."[66]

Although the hermit may be unfamiliar with the communal celebration of the liturgy, he embellishes himself nonetheless with psalmody, meditative reading, and vocal prayer: he has a liturgy all his own. The great hesychasts were perfectly aware of this: vocal prayer represented for them the pedagogy that must lead them to silent prayer, consisting of being simply present to God. To pray in the heart without ceasing, without any collaboration with the tongue, "this is the characteristic of the perfect, who are capable of directing their spirit and of keeping it in the fear of God. But the person who cannot unceasingly keep his spirit in the presence of God must, to the practice of the presence, add meditation and prayer of the lips."[67]

And Barsanuphius illustrates this with a parable:

> Consider those who swim in the sea: experienced swimmers dive into the water with assurance, knowing that the sea cannot engulf a good swimmer. By contrast, the one who is only beginning to learn, as soon as he feels himself sinking in the water, fearing asphyxiation, heads immediately for the shore.

[65] A Greek term that indicates independence and imperturbability with regard to passions and emotions.

[66] Barsanuphius and John of Gaza, Letter 182.

[67] Barsanuphius and John of Gaza, Letter 431.

Then, regaining a bit of courage, he once again immerses himself in the water. He thus makes multiple attempts in order to learn how to swim well, until he has attained the perfection of very experienced swimmers.[68]

One could scarcely describe better the activity or ascesis of one making progress toward the perfection of interior prayer. Whatever he does—whether he exerts himself to remain in absolute simplicity within the divine ocean or takes his repose on the beach of the Scriptures in meditation and psalmody—the hermit has but one occupation, one single preoccupation: being attentive to the liturgy of the Spirit in his heart.

In letter 74, John of Gaza traces the program of the hesychastic monk:

> The canonical hours and hymns are traditions: they are excellent for the purpose of common celebration by the people as well as in the *coenobia* because of the gathering of a great number.
>
> But the monks of Sketis[69] do not have hours nor do they chant hymns. All through the day they do have the work of their hands and meditation, both interrupted by short prayers.
>
> When you stand up to pray like them, you must invoke the Lord that you may be rid of the old man, or indeed you must say the Our Father, or even the two together, then sit down again to your manual work. You can prolong your prayer when you get up or you can pray without interruption, according to the precept of the Apostle, but to do so it is not necessary that you remain standing. For it is throughout the whole day that your spirit is at prayer. When you sit down to your manual work, you must recite by heart (*apostethizein*) or read the Psalms. At the end of each psalm, pray while remaining seated: "God, have pity on me, a wretch!" If you succumb to thoughts, add: "God, you see my oppression, help me!"
>
> When you have completed three rows of the prayer rope,[70] rise for the prayer, make a genuflection in the same fashion

[68] Barsanuphius and John of Gaza, Letter 431.

[69] Region south of Alexandria in Egypt, once populated by many hermits.

[70] One could also translate: "When you have worked at the rope for the duration of three *stichoi* of psalms . . ."

and, standing up again, offer the prayer you have just said. At Vespers, the dwellers of Sketis recite twelve psalms. At the end of each one they say the Alleluia instead of the doxology, and they offer a prayer. And the same holds true at night: twelve psalms, after which they sit for their manual work. If someone so desires he does recitation by heart; another examines his thoughts; yet another considers the lives of the Fathers. Whoever reads five or eight pages acquits himself of manual work. Whoever reads psalms or recites them by heart must do so with the lips (that is, aloud), unless there be another next to him and he wants no one to know what he is doing.[71]

One could hardly outline more clearly the occupation of the hesychast. Materially it is composed of a perfectly balanced succession of periods of manual work and more intense moments of prayer. This means that, in the depths of the heart, prayer and the solitary's presence to God never cease.

In the letter that we have just cited, the example of those who dwell in Sketis is twice held up. This is because here we are indeed retrieving a tradition born at the very origins of monasticism, and we could here cite more than one desert saying that illustrates the typically monastic rhythm of the life.[72] If continuous prayer does not animate this rhythm, the communal celebration of the liturgy loses its meaning:

Through the abba of the monastery he had in Palestine, Blessed Epiphanius, bishop of Cyprus, was informed of this: "Thanks to your prayers we neglect no rule; quite to the contrary, we recite with great care Terce, Sext, and None." Then Epiphanius

[71] Barsanuphius and John of Gaza, Letter 74.

[72] An Elder went to visit an old man of Sketis. Admiring his manner of life, he asked him how he had attained it. The old man replied: "I myself did not receive such a teaching from my fathers, but as you presently see me so have I been throughout my life: a little work, a little meditation, a little prayer and, insofar as I am able, I guard myself from thoughts and oppose those that present themselves to me. Thus, the spirit of contemplation came upon me without my knowing it." *Par questions et réponses, sur la façon dont il faut demeurer dans sa cellule et sur la contemplation*, n. 9, in *Apophthegmes des Pères du desert*, trad. J.-C.Guy (Textes de la Spiritualité Orientale, n. 1), ms. (Bégrolles-en-Mauges: Éditions de Bellefontaine), 419.

responded and offered them the following remark: "It is evident that you do not care about the other hours of the day, if you abstain from prayer. The true monk must, in fact, have prayer and psalmody continually in his heart."[73]

This text stands as categorical affirmation of the absolute necessity of a liturgical *beyond*, without which the common celebration loses all its value.

In conclusion we should stress that this manner of envisaging the synergy of liturgical and interior prayer must not be solely ascribed to the anachoretic or semianachoretic tradition. In the monasteries of Pachomius, whom we honor in modern times with the title of "founder of the *koinonia* or communal life," one discovers the same fundamental intuition. From his spiritual father, Abba Palamon, Pachomius receives a canon of prayer along with his initiation into monastic life: "As for the rule of the collect, sixty prayers per day and fifty per night, without counting the brief, spontaneous prayers we make so that we may not be liars, since we have been commanded to pray unceasingly."[74]

The Liturgy of the Gospel

In the secret place of our heart the Spirit of God builds the Church. It is there that he recapitulates us in Christ so that we may be holy and immaculate in love (Eph 1:4, 10), offering unceasingly to God continual acts of thanksgiving for the marvels he has accomplished in his Son.

It is he, the Spirit, who is "the pearl of great price" (Matt 13:46), "the hidden treasure" of the heart (Matt 13:44). It is he who is the seed of eternal life and the pledge of our glorification. It is he who is the author of our prayer, the uncreated light in which we are transformed, by whose strength we become capable of contemplating the face of the Lord.

---

[73] *Sayings*, Alphabetical Series, Epiphanius 3.

[74] *Life of Pachomius*, SBo (Sahidic-Bohairic text) 10; *Letter of Ammon* 348; quoted by A. Veilleux, "La liturgie dans le monachisme pachômien au IVème siècle," in *Studia Anselmiana* (Rome, 1968), 287–88.

Participating in this divine illumination we become "the image of the Image," according to the phrase of Saint Athanasius, and it is with unveiled faces that we radiate the glory of the Lord (2 Cor 3:18). It is, again, the Spirit who raises up in the Church, in keeping with the ineffable riches of his grace, the different ministries that serve the Word in its itinerary and build up the Body of Christ. As St. Paul famously states:

> To each one the manifestation of the Spirit is given in view of the common good. To one is given by the Spirit a word of wisdom; to another a word of knowledge according to the same Spirit; to another, faith by the same Spirit; to another the gift of healing by the same only Spirit; to another the power to work miracles; to another the gift of prophecy; to another the discernment of spirits is given; to another the gift of tongues; to another the gift of interpretation of tongues. But in all of these it is the same unique Spirit at work, distributing its gifts to each one in particular according to its intention. (1 Cor 12:7-11)

Such are the energies of the Spirit by which God himself gives testimony before the Church and the world. Such are the spiritual gifts, the charisms with which the Spirit decks out the Church, "like a bride adorned for her spouse" (Rev 21:2). Such is also the second aspect of the *beyond* of the liturgy. Created by the Spirit to be at the service of the Word, these gifts are the fruit of the growth of this Word in us. They make of us servants of the Word, coworkers with God in his work of salvation. They constitute by their marvelous variety and richness what we could call the *Liturgy of the Gospel*, in which each one exercises his ministry according to the grace received from the Spirit.

Like prayer, this Liturgy of the Gospel is also located alongside the communal celebration; but at the same time, it transcends it on every side. It precedes that celebration, for it calls, convokes, and gathers believers for the liturgical celebration in anticipation of the gathering of all the elect in the kingdom. It finds itself at the very heart of the celebration that, in its entirety, is the sacramental proclamation of the mystery of Christ. Beginning with this celebration and proceeding from it, the word of testimony spreads throughout the earth.

The whole New Testament attests to this conception, according to which the proclamation of the Word in all its dimensions is a veritable liturgy. The liturgy of the New Covenant is first enacted by Christ: "But now Christ has obtained a ministry [*leitourgia*] the more greatly exalted as the covenant of which he is the mediator is greater" (Heb 8:6). "We have a high-priest who has taken his seat at the right hand of the majesty in the heavens, minister [literally: *leitourgos*] of the sanctuary and of the true tabernacle, built not by man but by the Lord" (Heb 8:1-2). "By his saving work, Christ has reconciled all things to God, making peace by the blood of his cross" (Col 1:20).

The announcement of this salvation through the apostolic proclamation is itself one of the aspects of this new liturgy. In Christ it was God who reconciled the world to himself, and he placed on the lips of the apostles the message of reconciliation, confiding to them the ministry, the service of this reconciliation (2 Cor 5:18-19). Saint Paul, who was set apart to announce the Gospel of God (Rom 1:1), never ceases to call himself the minister of the Gospel (Col 1:23), "the minister of the Church in virtue of the charge that God has confided to me, to make known among you the advent of his Word, this mystery hidden from ages past . . . : that is, Christ among you, the hope of glory" (Col 1:25-27). The apostle is the minister of Jesus Christ, priest of the Gospel of God (Rom 15:16). It is thus that he fulfills the spiritual worship he owes to God: "God, whom I serve in my spirit in the Gospel of his Son" (Rom 1:9).

Purified of dead works by the shedding of the blood of Christ, Christians are consecrated to render worship to the living God (Heb 9:14). From that time on their whole life is to be a proclamation of the Gospel.[75] Thus, walking according to the Spirit, they

---

[75] "The whole life of a monk is preeminently invested with a liturgical character. . . . As in the case of martyrdom, this role is discharged more by the monk's being than by his action. It is in being what he is that the monk exercises an irreplaceable function in the Church, namely that of assuring the total reali-

offer themselves to God as a living sacrifice, holy and acceptable (Rom 12:1). And Saint Paul adds: "This is the spiritual worship that you must offer."

It is above all mainly by their fraternal charity that Christians bear witness to the Word of God: "By this they will know that you are my disciples, if you have love for one another" (John 13:35). This humble love for others, and especially for the poor, thus forms part of the evangelical witness: the least act of service is a liturgy because it carries within itself the manifestation of the mystery. Saint Paul, too, does not hesitate to use the name "liturgy" for the collection that he has organized for the Churches of Palestine: "The rendering of this service [*literally*: 'the service of this liturgy,' referring to the collection] not only supplies the wants of the saints but also overflows in many thanksgivings to God" (2 Cor 9:12; see also Rom 15:27).

As a manifestation of the plan of God, the Liturgy of the Gospel is not a human work. Just as with the Word offered in prayer, this witness and this service are above all a work of the Holy Spirit. We see in this the profound unity that exists between the *beyond* of the liturgical service in interior prayer and what we are calling here the Liturgy of the Gospel.

As we recall, the principle of this unity is the Holy Spirit himself. It is he who unites liturgical prayer and the liturgy of the heart into one spiritual activity. It is he who quickens the seed of the Word deposited in us, thereby realizing the mystery of our divinization. Again, it is he who testifies, by every sort of good work and by words of power, to the kingdom that accomplishes its parousia in us. From one end of Christian mystery to the other, it is the Spirit who accomplishes his work.

The Second Vatican Council, in its profound reflection on the Church, expressed magnificently the unity of this divine plan:

---

zation of the ideal preached by the hierarchy, the ideal of living in its fullness the reality produced and signified by the sacramental life of the Church. . . . He manifests in the Church the mystery of the *res* of the sacrament that the priest calls into being under the mystical symbol." S. Abhishiktesvarananda, "Le frère Monchanin," *La Vie spirituelle* 435 (1958): 71–95.

The Spirit dwells in the Church and in the hearts of the faithful, as in a temple (see 1 Cor 3:16; 6:19), prays and bears witness in them that they are his adopted children (see Gal 4:6; Rom 8:15-16 and 26). He guides the church in the way of all truth (see Jn 16:13) and, uniting it in fellowship and ministry, bestows upon it different hierarchic and charismatic gifts, and in this way directs it and adorns it with his fruits (see Eph 4:11-12; 1 Cor 12:4; Gal 5:22). By the power of the Gospel he rejuvenates the church, constantly renewing it and leading it to perfect union with its spouse. For the Spirit and the Bride both say to Jesus, the Lord, "Come!" (see Rev 22:17)[76]

The Witness of the Gospel and Spiritual Paternity

The monastic experience is perhaps one of the privileged arenas where the Word and the Liturgy of the Gospel are lived with the greatest spiritual intensity. We know that the written documents of the monastic tradition that we possess are nothing else than this witness to the transmission of the Word. The *apophthegmata*, in their very original form, describe for us the ministry of the Word which is the charism proper to the Desert Fathers. Indeed, we find here a necessary development clearly perceived by the Elders: in the relationship launched by spiritual paternity there takes place the most spiritual of events, namely, the transmission or *paradôsis* of the Word.

This necessity originates in our incapacity to understand Scripture, to perceive the Word of God in it and through our hearing of it. For this Word speaks to us the language of God that the natural person cannot perceive. Only the spiritual person, who is taught by the Spirit of God, knows the things of God and understands his Word (1 Cor 2:13-16).

The first step of the monk is therefore to recognize our deep-seated natural inability:

Some old men came one day to Abba Antony, and Abba Joseph was among them. Wishing to test them, the old man proposed to them a word of Scripture and, beginning with the young-

---

[76] *Lumen Gentium* 4.

est, asked them the meaning of this word. And each of them spoke according to his ability. But to each one the old man said: "You have not discovered it." Last of all he said to Abba Joseph: "You, how do you explain this word?" He responded: "I do not know." Then Abba Antony said: "Truly, Abba Joseph has found the way, for he said: 'I do not know.'"[77]

The second step is of greater importance. While persevering in hope and imploring unceasingly the grace of the Spirit, the novice must devote himself through attentive listening to a Spirit-bearing father from whom he will receive the Word.

A spiritual father is not simply an Elder whose task it is to educate young monks in their initiation to a wisdom for living; still less is he a tutor charged with ensuring some sort of intellectual formation. He is a man who, filled with the power of the Spirit, has become the prophet of God. Through the coming of the Spirit into his heart, he is filled with the power to proclaim the Word.[78]

Such is undoubtedly the charism proper to spiritual paternity:

Some brothers who had with them some seculars came to see Abba Felix and they begged him to speak a word to them. But the old man kept silent. After they had pleaded with him a long time, he said to them: "Do you want to hear a word?" They said: "Yes, abba!" The old man then said to them: "From

---

[77] *Sayings*, Alphabetical Series, Antony 17.

[78] "The *pneuma* appears as the authentic fruit of monastic life. 'Shed your blood and receive the *pneuma*': this *rhêma* or 'pneumatic word' explains briefly and adequately the foundational reality of monasticism. Whoever has committed himself to follow the Lord and has died to the world, whoever has sacrificed his 'blood,' that is to say, the vital force of the natural, earthly man—such a one has attained to a new life that is a participation in the divine life itself. Asceticism, humility, renunciation of self, perpetual prayer, and reading of the Word of God: all *anachôrêsis* has no meaning if it does not lead to this participation. This is why the perfect monk is essentially an 'abba,' that is to say, a Spirit-bearer, one who bears the divine *pneuma* or vital breath, who is filled above all with this force and can communicate it in his turn in such wise that he becomes a spiritual father who, like Saint Paul, bears testimony in Christ Jesus." Odo Casel, "Mönchtum und Pneuma," *Morgenländisches Christentum* (1940): 326; quoted from *Théologie de la vie monastique d'après quelques grands moines des époques moderne et contemporaine* (Ligugé: Abbaye Saint-Martin, 1961), 169.

now on there are no more words. When the brothers questioned the old men and carried out what was said to them, God would show the old men how to speak. But now, since they question without putting into practice what they hear, God has withdrawn from the old men the grace of the Word and they no longer find anything to say inasmuch as there are no more workers.[79]

Let there be no mistake about the importance of this transmission of the Word. It extends to us the creative Word that brought the universe into being. It is the echo of the first word that God cried out over the world, on the day when he made light emerge from the darkness. Three times happy is the one who has heard with his own ears the Word of the beginning from the mouth of his spiritual father:

All the words that, through the Spirit, issue from the mouths of the saints are but one Word that comes from the mouth of God. Such is the savory inspiration of the Spirit in all its power: not all taste of it, but only those who are worthy of it. There are indeed but few who rejoice unceasingly in the things of the Spirit. Most content themselves with images (*typoi*) of the spiritual words that they know and in which they participate by remembrance. But they do not yet possess the true bread that is to come: the sensory experience of the Word of God. In that experience the Word alone stands before us as the source of all joy for those who are found worthy. It is never absorbed, never depleted, never consumed.[80]

To fulfill this function, or rather to accomplish this work, the monk has received from the Spirit a gift, the charism of discernment or *diakrisis*. The great Antony did not hesitate to make of it the monastic virtue par excellence, the flower that the Spirit causes to bloom in the desert: "Someone asked an old man: 'What is the work of the monk?' He responded: 'Discernment.'"[81]

---

[79] *Sayings*, Alphabetical Series, Felix 1.
[80] Gregory of Sinai, excerpt from *Acrostics on the Commandments*.
[81] *Sayings of Those Who Grew Old in Their Practice* 9.

Discernment, a power of the Spirit that shines beyond all shadows, reveals to us the will of God. It is the lamp for our steps on our way to the Lord, causing us to know the will of God in all knowledge and wisdom. This will is not situated first of all on the level of moral conduct but rather on the level of being and creation. The will of God is first of all that the other may *be*, that the other may exist. This work of discernment will also pertain to the discovery of the spiritual face of this new creature in Christ. It requires that, by the grace of the Spirit, the spiritual father open the eyes of his son and make him discover the mystery that resides within him. In the light of this revelation, the disciple is enabled to gain access to his full spiritual maturity. This presupposes a long road on which to make the journey together, the road that Saint Benedict traced before us with so much realism: the road that crosses the desert of humility.[82]

By virtue of this new birth, the monk has been established with absolute certitude in his spiritual identity as a son of God and thus he has in truth become a spiritual man, an icon of the Lord whom he contemplates in his heart. He has in his turn become capable of transmitting life, of bearing the Word and, if God should give him the grace, of crying out over a new being this Word of creation.

"Fathers of All Humanity"

Ought the preeminent role played by spiritual paternity within the monastic charism go beyond the confines of the desert? At first glance, there seems to be no obstacle to such expansion and everything seems to suggest it. Is it not this discernment that generates a life meant for the entire people of God? And why not?

In actual fact, however, not all monks are called to this; not all are destined to exercise concretely a spiritual paternity. The Word of God is never chained; it evolves in perfect freedom, blazes its own trail in the hearts and lives of those whom it has claimed as its own. We have seen how it can invest one's whole

---

[82] See RB 7.

life through the interior liturgy of prayer. Others are called by the Word to celebrate, in one way or another, the liturgy of the *kerygma*. No one would be able to assess his own option, or judge that of another, without first having been totally transformed by the Spirit and thus become the intimate confidant of the Word.

Certain monastic milieus have remained very reticent toward any diffusion of the Word beyond their confines. We ought to respect this grace in the measure that it bears the mark of the Spirit:

> Having received a personal invitation from the Emperor Constans to come to Constantinople to meet him, Antony questioned one of his disciples, Abba Paul: "Should I go?" The latter responded: "If you leave, people will call you Antony, if you do not leave, Abba Antony."[83]

True paternity, authentic *abbacy* in the ancient sense of the word, can scarcely exist apart from the sign of concrete life in the desert, with all the renunciations it implies, and this is a sign that we must always try to show forth in the most rigorous and transparent manner.

The direct opposite of this at times fierce reserve is found in those others who have lent themselves to the invitations that the Spirit has sown along their way. Antony himself left his solitude in order to give witness at Alexandria at the moment of persecution. In the same way Julian Saba went down to Constantinople at the time of the sedition of 387: "Everyone fled, but the men who feared God, those who lived in monasteries, did not fear to hasten to the scene."[84]

Nothing can prevent the monk from bearing witness when his hour has come and the Spirit impels him. Certainly today a greater liberty is called for to allow all opportunities for this liturgy of witness. But still more do we need true spiritual discernment, which alone can preserve from illusion the monk who assumes responsibility for the Word.

---

[83] *Sayings*, Alphabetical Series, Antony 31.
[84] John Chrysostom, *Homily to the People of Antioch* 18.4 (*PG* 49, 186).

Let us return for a moment to *The Book of Steps*. We see described there a form of premonastic life that unites in one marvelous synthesis the liturgy of the heart and the witness of the Gospel. As we have already pointed out, the book's addressees are men devoted exclusively to prayer and teaching. In this they succeed the apostles who, in establishing deacons, reserved to themselves the ministry of the Word and of prayer.[85]

The interior liturgy of the heart, so important in *The Book of Steps*, is always accompanied by an exterior liturgy, a ministry at the service of others. This latter can, in addition, be either corporal or spiritual and, when accompanied and sustained by prayer, is properly a work of discernment and exhortation:

> The Lord demands of those who are in the Spirit that they cling to him by constant meditation, by the sacrifice of their innermost heart, by praise, and by prayer and humility, while at the same time they spend themselves in discernment for the instruction of every man.

And note the description of the instruction that follows the above, adapted to the spiritual possibilities of each person:

> Just as the Spirit teaches them, so they in turn instruct others in humility and make of each man a servant of God, according to the possibility of each. Let them make into a spiritual man whoever can serve in the Spirit. Let them teach how to serve the Lord corporally whoever can serve with his body. . . . The spiritual servants [or deacons] discern the commandments, teach the true Word and show every man how to live and grow.[86]

A final aspect of this spiritual diaconate brings it still closer to the liturgical celebration. In the fullness of charity it becomes a prayer of intercession for all humanity:

> The love of perfection possesses nothing but the clothing and the food of the day. It desires nothing earthly. . . . [The

---

[85] Acts 6:4, cited in LG 3.7.15.
[86] LG 3.14.

spiritual deacon] teaches and does good to every person in words of truth and certitude, and he makes himself the servant of everyone in love. He exhorts some and instructs others. He loves and respects all and prays for all. . . . His spirit clings to our Father who is in heaven. At every hour and in every place he gives thanks and glory. For perfect love cannot help but love every human being nor can it cease praying for all.[87]

Intercession on behalf of every human being and of the whole universe thus emerges as the final fruit of the Word, and it is in this fruit that the *apostolic* vocation of the monk and of all Christians culminates. "They give thanks on behalf of the entire universe as if they were the fathers of humanity," remarked John Chrysostom in their regard.[88] And, furthermore, "they pray for the universe, this being the greatest testimony to their friendship,"[89] "for the immense kindness of the Lord knows very well how to grant salvation to the mass of humanity because of a few just men."[90]

In monastic life, the Word is thus called to unfold all its possibilities, to complete its course, to realize itself in full: angelic praise, witness of martyrs, triumph of the kingdom. Saint John Chrysostom again attests to this in a famous passage:

If you go now to the desert of Egypt, it will appear to your eyes like the most marvelous paradise with its thousands of angelic choirs with human faces, its crowds of martyrs, its assemblies of virgins: there you will see the tyranny of the demon brought to nought and the kingdom of Christ in its splendor.[91]

Conclusion

We have attempted to describe the progress of the Word first of all in the human heart, then through the structure of the Church, be-

[87] LG 13.7.
[88] John Chrysostom, *Homily on the Gospel of Matthew* 55.5, PG 58, 547.
[89] John Chrysostom, *Homily on the Gospel of John* 78.4, PG 59, 426.
[90] John Chrysostom, *Homily on Genesis* 42.5, PG 54, 392.
[91] John Chrysostom, *Homily on the Gospel of Matthew* 8.4, PG 57, 87.

fore it finally returns to God on the completion of its mission. The Word indeed exceeds the context of the celebration. It emerges as a powerful principle of unity for all Christian experience. It is within this Word that the *beyond* of the liturgy is grounded. The structure of the Word of God and that of the liturgy harmonize well: the one is created *for* the other because the one is created *by* the other.

The liturgy can never enclose the Word within its structures. The latter must remain open so that all the promises contained within the Word of God may flower and unfold in the life of Christians and of the Church. Where this does not take place, the liturgical assembly remains sterile.

The Word, received in the liturgical assembly, bears fruit in different directions. Listened to in silence, assimilated by a pure heart, the Word is returned to God in prayer. This essential structure of the Word is also that of the liturgical celebration. It is already present there in seed form. Beyond the public and communal celebration, the Word seeks to bloom in a *sacrificium privatum*, or in the *kryptê ergasía* or "hidden work" of the heart. This is the interior, hidden work of the Word that, welcomed into the innermost heart, mysteriously becomes perpetual prayer and the activity of grace: the exercise of the spiritual priesthood performed by the monk who, without growing weary, offers a sacrifice of praise on the altar of his heart.

Since on all sides the structures are ordered to the same prayer, to the same flowering of the Word, there is no opposition but rather perfect continuity between the liturgical celebration and contemplative prayer. The liturgy is ordered to interior prayer like the seed to its fruit. The practice of such contemplative prayer, as detached from the communal celebration as it may appear, is nothing other than the progressive interiorization of an event and a rhythm first experienced at the level of fraternal communion. It is a progressive assumption by the Word, or rather it is the Word's claiming for itself a pure and naked heart, called to continue the dialogue with the Father in the Spirit.

This "fruit of lips that confess his Name" (Heb 13:15) is not only offered to God. It appears also in the witness—the "tradition," or transmission—of the Word to one's brothers and sisters. It is in contemplative prayer and, at the same time, in apostolic witness that the monk, thanks to the Word, is called to become a *speaker in tongues* and a *prophet*, to use these terms in the very precise sense they bear in the New Testament. This transpires first of all with regard to the monastic community itself. At the heart of the Church, this community is the firstfruits of the Word proclaimed in its bosom, called together and constituted entirely by this Word addressed to it in the desert.

The liturgical proclamation of the Word exists here parallel to the transmission of the *rhêma*, of the *apophthegm* of the Fathers, of the Word given "so that my heart may live," a transmission that constitutes spiritual paternity. Perhaps no other ecclesial space exists where the eternal fruitfulness and efficacy of the Word of God may be experienced so forcefully. After having learned to discern and welcome the Word as a son, each monk is normally called to become an *abba*, to engender other sons in turn, thanks to the Word. This paternity in both the sharing of the Word and in the intercession offered by the *abba* on behalf of his sons is fundamentally liturgical. The spiritual father becomes the liturgical celebrant par excellence, accomplishing in the whole of his life what is sacramentally represented in the liturgical *synaxis*.

This prophetic role of the monk does not stop at the borders of the desert. He can discharge it in such a manner that people will come running to him from afar, probably more numerous than he would ever wish.

It can also happen that the monk, conscious of having received a mission from the Lord, sometimes consents to bear his testimony before the whole Church, yet not without having first of all been willing to go, so to speak, to the farthest confines of the desert, and after having there received the Spirit and been initiated into the Word.

The word of the monk will always remain marked by its prophetic origins, by the crucible in which it has been purified in him. It will proclaim a preference for breaking with the world that is passing away and for the often abrupt urgency of the kingdom that is near.

From one end to the other of this process of flourishing—first liturgical, then metaliturgical—we see how perfect are the unity and continuity of the Word in both spheres in the eyes of the person who draws life from them. Such a person feels neither opposition nor collision but rather a tranquil progression of life, a fertile going-beyond that does not deny the preceding steps but assumes them every time into a new unity and harmony. The *opus Dei*, in all the primitive scope of the term, melds more and more with all the activities of the monk and becomes coextensive with his life. Not only does he prefer nothing to the work of God[92] but also, all the life of the monk has been transformed into liturgy, has become one unceasing *opus Dei*.[93]

[92] RB 43.3.
[93] Sulpice Sévère, *Vie de saint Martin*, Sources chrétiennes 133 (Paris: Éditions du Cerf, 1967).

12

If You Want to See, You Have to Love

The mystery of Jesus dead and risen is not visible except to the eyes of one who loves.

Already at Calvary, Jesus was surrounded by those who loved him. There were three: John, the disciple whom Jesus loved; Mary, his mother; and Mary Magdalene. They had endured the evening and the night, they had come to the end of the shock caused by the arrest of Jesus in the garden, they had lived through the insistent suspicions of the servant girl who precipitated Peter's fall and the brutality of the soldiers all along the procession of the condemned, to arrive finally where they find themselves now, on Calvary, standing beneath the cross of Jesus. If they have borne all of the above it is now no longer so that they can receive the love of Jesus but, on the contrary, so that they can give him theirs by surrounding his agony and death with every possible human tenderness.

There was first of all Mary, his mother, the woman who once could envelop him with love while he was still a tiny child. It was her joy to snuggle him and bury him in a mother's sweetest caresses. It was she, too, who received him again for a few instants on her knees, up against her heart, to rock him to sleep one last time—this same body, flesh of her flesh—but rock him now with her tears and songs of sorrow, entrusting him to the slumber of death.

Then there is Mary Magdalene, the repentant sinner, she who loved Jesus so much that on one beautiful day all her sins were forgiven her at once. Our Latin liturgy conflates her—happily, I would say—with the other Mary, the one from Bethany, of whom John often recalls how greatly Jesus loved her. But both of them, one day, received the favor of washing the feet of Jesus, just as his mother had once done for him, and both dared to wipe his feet with their superb tresses and anoint them with precious perfume. Jesus could very well have wanted to confide in advance the task of his coming burial to the love of these two women, since it was with reference to that love, as he specified, that they had performed so precious an unction.

Then there is John, the mysterious disciple especially loved by Jesus who, while reclining at table next to Jesus, had taken the liberty to lean back and rest a moment "on his breast," as notes the author of the Fourth Gospel, again using the very words with which, in his prologue, he had described the Word equally nestled "in the bosom of the Father." For Jesus this was a very moving symbol at once of the love he had received from all eternity from the Father and of the love he gives to his friends here below.

In his last hour only the love of these three has followed Jesus, surrounding him with infinite tenderness at the moment when he is going to slip away in slumber, in order to pass from one love to the other, from the fragile signs here below to the overflowing reality beyond, but always the same one and only love. Before thus handing himself over, however, Jesus must still devise a final act of love, the only one of which he is capable now, suspended on the cross. Seeing his mother, and next to her the disciple whom he loved, Jesus says to his mother: "Woman, behold your son." Then he says to his disciple: "Behold your mother." Now the end can come for Jesus as a real accomplishment. Love has exhausted him and he has exhausted all love. The moment has come when he can go beyond this threefold human tenderness that has obstinately accompanied him up to this point: the infinite gentleness of a mother, the ardent passion of the sinner whom love has healed, and the tender attachment of the brother marked out with special fondness. Before Jesus surrenders and falls asleep into the other love, the Love beyond, nothing remains for him but to gently detach these dear ones from himself so as to give them to one another as a sign of farewell and eternal remembrance. His mother receives a new son, who was the favorite son of Jesus. The disciple receives a new mother, who was the sole mother of Jesus.

From this moment on all is fulfilled: the Scriptures, first of all, but also the long trajectory of love to the very end, the love that Jesus gave, the love that he received. He can now incline his head and surrender his spirit to his Father. His last breath is also a kiss, the very first kiss and now the eternal kiss of the love beyond: of the Word in the embrace of the Father. Ever since the death of Jesus, which was for the first time a death-in-love, every death resembles his: it is a Passover, that is to say, the passage from one love to the other, from the signs to the reality. Every death can henceforth be like that of Jesus, who let himself be cradled by so much love, who let himself fall asleep in death, or in love—it is all one—tight against the Father's breast.

At dawn on Easter we again find hearts that love and alone can understand the wildly unexpected message: "He is risen from the dead." Death is no more. The death of Jesus was his victory over death, once for all. Jesus is henceforth the Living One forever.

His victory over death . . . But why and how? Simply because it was a death out of love. As the Letter to the Hebrews says, it was "because of his filial love" that the loud cries and tears offered by Jesus during his Passion were favorably heard. At the sight of his Child, crucified out of love, the Father was moved by gut-wrenching compassion. God could not resist. As the psalmist had foretold: "He could not abandon him to death, nor let his beloved see corruption" (Ps 15:10). It is love that has demolished the gates of death and caused the Living One to spring forth from the tomb.

Because it is the masterpiece of love, Easter is not directly visible except to the eyes of love. The message of the resurrection is entrusted first of all to those who are close to Jesus, to those who have loved him or have been loved by him, as if that message would become too fragile in other hands. Even the apostles are not its first witnesses, though they would later become *the* accredited witnesses of the risen Jesus. But they were not so from the start. Would they have recognized Jesus? Or would they have imagined they were seeing a ghost, as in the tempest on the lake?

In any case, the firstfruits of the resurrection are reserved to those who know how to gaze with their heart and who, for this reason, see what others are not yet able to see.

First among these seers were the holy women, and first among them was Mary Magdalene. The women disciples did not doubt for a single instant. An apostle, standing before the empty tomb, would have examined the places and circumstances and demanded proofs. The women, on the contrary, at once give credence to the angel's words and, already trembling with emotion and full of joy, run to transmit the news to the apostles who, for their part, receive them coldly as "gossipy women," as Saint Luke notes. One more beautiful surprise still lies in wait for Mary Magdalene. At the very instant when an unknown person pronounces her name in the garden and she hears "Mary," she recognizes Jesus. And why? Solely because of the accent of love with which Jesus pronounced her name and because of her own desire suddenly overflowing. Indeed, is there any sweeter connection between two persons who love each other than their names, spoken in a certain unique and inimitable fashion? And what clearer proof of his resurrection than this could be expected by one who loves Jesus? Her mere name, pronounced with all the gentleness of love, surpassed all other proofs.

Among the apostles there was only one exception. This was, of course, John, the disciple closest to Jesus, someone who already understood while the others still doubted, someone who recognized Jesus when the others still saw nothing. In recognizing Jesus, love always arrives first. Peter had entered before John into the empty tomb. The spectacle had astonished him, troubled him, but nothing more. John entered after him, and "he saw and believed" at that very moment, says the gospel. In the same way, John again anticipates all the others when they encountered the stranger frying fish on the shore after a night of futile fishing on their part. By instinct he guessed it: "It is the Lord."

Love was first to recognize the risen Jesus. It is still love that promises all of us that we will see him in turn: "Go, and say to my brothers that they must go to Galilee [that is to say, they must return to their homes and to their work]. There they will see me"

(Matt 28:10). We dare give credit to the love of Mary Magdalene and the love of John because only love is credible—their love and ours. Our love may yet be in its infancy, always exposed to dangers. But this does not much matter, for there it is nonetheless in its littleness and humility. And for love a little is already a lot. The sweet name of the risen Jesus, in our heart and on our lips, and our name, whispered by him in the ear of our heart, surpass all other proofs.

Sources

1. *Spiritual Experience*
Originally presented to major superiors in Belgium, this English text was used as a preparatory paper for the second Asian Monastic Congress. It first appeared in print in *Cistercian Studies* 2 (1975) and has been slightly adapted for this book.

2. *The Contemplative Life:*
Conference given at Rome in November 1993, during a meeting of superiors general, in preparation for the Synod on Religious Life.

3. *The Common Life: A School of Charity*
This text appears here for the first time.

4. *Living in a Fraternal Community*
Vie consacrée 3 (1984) : 135–52.

5. *Obedience in the Monastic Tradition*
Vie consacrée 4 (1976) : 197–210.

6. *Apostolic and Contemplative Dimensions of Religious Life*
Vie consacrée 3 (1985): 147–64. This conference, cast in the oral style, was given in November 1983 at the National Meeting of Episcopal Vicars for the Religious Institutes of France.

7. *In Solidarity*
Collectanea Cisterciensia 2 (1973): 143–48. This was the intervention of Dom André Louf at the General Assembly of Major Superiors of France (Paris, November 14–16, 1972). The spontaneity of the oral style has been retained.

8. *Notes from a Pilgrimage*
Collectanea Cisterciensia 1 (1970): 44–46.

9. *Monks and Ecumenism*
Collectanea Cisterciensia 3 (1982): 169–82. Conference given at Paris on June 11, 1980, in the Anglican Church of Saint George, as part of the celebration of the fifteenth centenary of the birth of Saint Benedict, at the end of the general assembly of the Association for the Unity of Christians.

10. *In the School of the Psalms*
Christus 96 (1977): 148–64.

11. *The Word beyond the Liturgy*
Conference given on July 4, 1969, at the fourth session of "Liturgie et Monastère," at the Belgian monastery of Wavreumont.

12. *If You Want to See, You Have to Love*
Les Amis du monastère 94 (1993).